2

LUCY LARCOM
LIFE, LETTERS, AND DIARY

BY

DANIEL DULANY ADDISON

BOSTON AND NEW YORK
HOUGHTON, MIFFLIN AND COMPANY
The Riverside Press, Cambridge
1895

The Riverside Press, Cambridge, Mass., U. S. A.
Electrotyped and Printed by H. O. Houghton & Co.

PREFACE.

It was the purpose of Miss Larcom to write a sequel to her book, "A New England Girlhood," in which she intended to give some account of her life in the log-cabins on the Western prairies as a pioneer and schoolmistress, and her experiences as a teacher in Wheaton Seminary, and as an editor and literary woman. She also wished to trace the growth of her religious ideas by showing the process through which she was led to undergo changes that finally made her accept a less rigorous theology than the one in which she had been reared. Her fascinating style, with its wealth of reminiscence and interesting detail, would have characterized her later book, as it did the former, but she died before beginning it, and American literature has lost a valuable record of a woman's life. A keen observer, her contact with famous men and women gave her an opportunity for a large knowledge of persons and events; deeply interested in the questions of the day, her comments would have been just and luminous; and her sensitiveness to impressions was such that the varied influences upon her life would have been most attractively presented. She was deeply spiritual, and the account of her religious experiences would have supplemented the moral power of her published works; but she was not permitted to give us, in autobiographical form, the rich fruits of a well-spent life.

The only preparation she had made for this book was a few notes suggesting a title and headings of the chapters. She proposed naming it, "Hitherward: A Life-Path Retraced." The suggestions for chapters indicate the subjects that she intended to treat, — "The Charm of Elsewhere;" "Over the Prairies;" "Log-Cabin Experiences;" "A Pioneer Schoolmistress;" "Teacher and Student;" Back to the Bay State;" "Undercurrents;" "Beneath Norton Elms;" "During the War;" "With 'Our Young Folks;'" "Successful Failures;" and "Going On."

After her death, her papers came into my possession. An examination showed that there was material enough in her letters and diary to preserve still some record of her later life, and possibly to continue the narrative which she had given in "A New England Girlhood."

It will be noticed that some years are treated more at length than others, the reason for this being that more data have been accessible for those periods; and also, as is the case with most lives, there were epochs of intenser emotion, more lasting experiences, and deeper friendships, the account of which is of greater value to the general reader than the more commonplace incidents of her career.

Her life was one of thought, not of action. In their outward movement, her days flowed on very smoothly. She had no remarkable adventures; but she had a constant succession of mental vicissitudes, which are often more dramatic and real than the outward events of even a varied life. In her loves and sympathies, in her philosophy of living and her creed, in her literary labors, — her poetry and her prose, — in her studies of man, nature, and God, she revealed a mind continually venturing into the known and unknown, and bringing back trophies of struggles and victories, of doubts and beliefs, of despair and faith. My aim has been to present the character of a New England woman, as it was thus moulded by the intellectual and moral forces of American living for the last fifty years; and to show how she absorbed the best from all sides, and responded to the highest influences.

There are passages in her diaries that remind one of Pascal's "Thoughts," for their frankness and spiritual depth; there are others that recall Amiel's Journal, with its record of emotions and longings after light. If such a singularly transparent and pure life had preserved for us its inner history, it would be more valuable than any record of mere outward events. Some such inner history I have attempted to give, by making selections from her journal and letters; and if, at times, I have allowed her inmost thoughts and motives to be disclosed, it has been with the feeling that such frankness would be helpful in portraying a soul stirred with love for the beautiful, a heart loving humanity, a spirit with the passion for God in it. She once said, "I am willing to make any part of my life public, if it will help others."

One soon sees that the religious element predominated in her character. From her earliest years, these questions of the soul's relation to man, to nature, and to God were uppermost in her mind. She was impelled to master them; and as Jacob wrestled with the angel, she could not let Life go until she had received from it a blessing. She found her rest and comfort in a Christianity which had its centre in no theory or dogma, no ecclesiastical system, but in the person of Jesus. For Him she had the most loyal love. He satisfied her soul; He interpreted life for her; He gave her the inspiration for her work; and with this belief, she went forth to live and to die, having the hope and confidence of a larger life beyond.

She was a prophetess to her generation, singing

the songs of a newer faith, and breathing forth in hymns and lyrics, and even homely ballads, her belief in God and immortality. Her two books, "As It Is in Heaven" and "The Unseen Friend," written in the last years of her life, when she had felt the presence of an invisible Power, and had caught glimpses of the spiritual world through the intimations of happiness given her in this life, are messages to human souls, that come with authority, and mark her as a strong spiritual force in our American Christianity. She will be known, I feel, not only as a woman with the most delicate perceptions of the sweetness of truth, and an appreciation of its poetry, but as one who could grasp the eternal facts out of the infinite, and clothe them with such beauty of imagery, and softness of music, that other lives could receive from her a blessing.

I must make public acknowledgment to those who have willingly rendered me assistance, — to Miss Lucy Larcom Spaulding (now Mrs. Clark), who gave me the privilege of using the rich material her aunt had left in her guardianship; to Mrs. James Guild, who furnished me with facts of great interest; to Mrs. I. W. Baker, the sister of Miss Larcom, whose advice has proved most valuable; to Miss Susan Hayes Ward, who put at my disposal the material used in the Memorial Number of "The Rushlight," the magazine of Wheaton Seminary; to Mr. S. T. Pickard, for permitting me to use some of Mr. Whittier's letters; to the Rev. Arthur Brooks, D. D., who consented to my using the letters of his brother, Bishop Brooks; to Prof. George E. Woodberry, whose sympathy and suggestions have been of the greatest service to me; and to all who have loaned the letters that so clearly illustrate the richness of Miss Larcom's personality.

DANIEL DULANY ADDISON.

Beverly, Mass., June 19, 1894.

CONTENTS.

LUCY LARCOM.

CHAPTER I.

EARLY DAYS.

1824–1846.

Lucy Larcom was born on March 5, 1824, in the old seaside town of Beverly, Massachusetts. She was next to the youngest in a family of seven sisters and two brothers. Her father, Benjamin Larcom, a retired shipmaster who became a shopkeeper selling West India goods, was a man of strong natural ability, and her mother, Lois Barrett, "with bright blue eyes and soft dark curling hair, which she kept pinned up under her white lace cap," was known for her sweetness. The Larcoms had lived for generations on the borders of the sea. Mordecai Larcom, born 1629, appeared in Ipswich in 1655, and soon after moved to Beverly, where he obtained a grant of land. His son, Cornelius Larcom, born 1658, purchased a place on the coast, in what is known as Beverly Farms. David Larcom was born 1701, and his son, Jonathan, born 1742, was the grandfather of Miss Larcom. The qualities of energy and self-reliance that come from the cultivation of Essex County soil and the winning of a livelihood as trader and sailor, were apparent in the branch of the family that lived in Wallace Lane, — one of the by-streets of the quaint village, that led in one direction through the fields to Bass River, "running with its tidal water from inland hills," and in the other across the main street to the harbor, with its fishing schooners and glimpses of the sea.

Her sensitive nature quickly responded to the free surroundings of her childhood. The open fields with the wild flowers and granite ledges covered with vines, and the sandy beaches of the harbor, and the village streets with their quiet picturesque life, formed her playground. The little daily events happening around her were interesting: the stage-coach rattling down Cabot Street; the arrival of a ship returning from a distant voyage; the stately equipage driven from the doorway of Colonel Thorndike's house; the Sunday services in the meeting-house; the companionship of other children, and the charm of her simple home life. These experiences are graphically recorded in "A New England Girlhood," where she testifies to her love for her native town. "There is something in the place where we were born that holds us always by the heart-strings. A town that has a great deal of country in it, one that is rich in beautiful scenery and ancestral associations, is almost like a living being, with a body and a soul. We speak of such a town as of a mother, and think of ourselves as her sons and daughters. So we felt about our dear native town of Beverly."

In her poems there are numerous references to the town: —

"Steady we 'll scud by the Cape Ann shore,
Then back to the Beverly Bells once more.
The Beverly Bells
Ring to the tide as it ebbs and swells."

In another place she says: —

"The gleam of
Thacher's Isle, twin-beaconed, winking back
To twinkling sister-eyes of Baker's Isle."

Her childhood was a period which she always looked back upon with fondness, for the deep impressions made upon her mind never were obliterated. The continued possession of these happy remembrances as she incorporated them into her womanhood, is shown by the way she entered into the lives of other children, whether in compiling a book of poems, like "Child Life," known wherever there are nurseries, or in writing her own book, "Childhood Songs," or in some of her many sketches in "Our Young Folks," "St. Nicholas," or the "Youth's Companion." She knew by an unerring instinct what children were thinking about, and how to interest them. She always took delight in the little rivulets in the fields, or the brown thrush singing from the tree, or the pussy-clover running wild, and eagerly watched for the red-letter days of children, the anniversaries and birthdays. She had happy memories of play in the old roomy barn, and of the improvised swing hung from the rafters. She recalled the fairy-tales and wonderful stories to which she listened with wide open eyes; the reflection of her face in the burnished brass of the tongs; and her child's night-thoughts when she began to feel that there were mysteries around her, and to remember that the stars were shining when she was tucked in bed.

Lucy Larcom's book-learning began very early. It seems almost incredible that she should have been able to read at two and a half years of age, but such is the general testimony of her family. She used to sit by the side of her old Aunt Stanley, and thread needles for her, listening to the songs and stories that the old lady told; and Aunt Hannah, in the school held in her kitchen, where she often let the children taste the good things that were cooking, managed not only to keep her out of mischief, by her "pudding-stick" ferule, or by rapping her on the head with a thimble, but taught her the "a, b, abs," and parts of the Psalms and Epistles.

The strongest influence in her development was that of her sister Emeline, who inspired her with love for knowledge, and instilled in her the highest ideals of girlhood. This sister supplied her, as she grew older, with books, and guided her reading. Referring to this, she once said: —

"I wish to give due credit to my earliest educators, — those time-stained, thumb-worn books, that made me aware of living in a world of natural grandeur, of lofty visions, of heroic achievements, of human faithfulness, and sacrifice. I always feel like entering a protest when I hear people say that there was very little for children to read fifty years ago. There was very little of the cake and confectionery style of literature, which is so abundant now; but we had the genuine thing, — solid food, in small quantities, to suit our capacity, — and I think we were better off for not having too much of the lighter sort. What we had 'stayed by.'"

The books that she read were "Pilgrim's Progress," "Paul and Virginia," "Gulliver's Travels," Sir Walter Scott's novels; and in poetry, Spenser, Southey, Wordsworth, and Coleridge. She knew these volumes almost by heart.

Lucy's first love for poetry was fostered by the hymns she used to read in church, during sermon time, when the minister from his lofty pulpit entered upon a series of "finallys," which did not seem to be meant for her. Her fondness for hymns was so great that at one time she learned a hundred. The rhythm of the musical accompaniment and the flow of the words taught her the measured feet of verse before she ever heard of an iambus or a choriambus. Finding that her own thoughts naturally expressed themselves in rhyme, she used frequently to write little verses, and stuff them down the crack in the floor of the attic. The first poem that she read to the family was long remembered by them, as, wriggling with embarrassment, she sat on a stool. Referring to her poetry at this time, she says, "I wrote little verses, to be sure, but that was nothing; they just grew. They were the same as breathing or singing. I could not help writing them. They seemed to fly into my mind like birds going with a carol through the air."

There is an incident worth repeating, that illustrates her sweetness and thoughtfulness of others. When her father died, she tried to comfort her mother: "I felt like preaching to her, but I was too small a child to do that; so I did the next best thing I could think of, — I sang hymns, as if singing to myself, while I meant them for her."

These happy days in the country village came to an end in the year 1835, when necessity forced Mrs. Larcom, after the death of her husband, to seek a home in the manufacturing community of Lowell, where there were more opportunities for the various members of her family to assist in the general maintenance of the home.

In Lowell, there were corporation boarding-houses for the operatives, requiring respectable matrons as housekeepers, and positions in the mills offered a means of livelihood to young girls. Attracted by these inducements, many New England families left their homes, in the mountains of New Hampshire and along the seacoast, and went to Lowell. The class of the employees in the mills was consequently different from the ordinary factory hand of to-day. Girls of education and refinement, who had no idea of remaining in a mill all their lives, worked in them for some years with the object, often, of helping to send a brother to college or making money enough to continue their education, or to aid dear ones who had been left suddenly without support: —

> "Not always to be here among the looms, —
> Scarcely a girl she knew expected that;
> Means to one end, their labor was, — to put
> Gold nest-eggs in the bank, or to redeem
> A mortgaged homestead, or to pay the way
> Through classic years at some academy;
> More commonly to lay a dowry by
> For future housekeeping."[1]

The intention of Mr. Francis Cabot Lowell and Mr. Nathan Appleton, when they conceived the idea of establishing the mills, was to provide conditions of living for operatives, as different as possible from the Old World ideals of factory labor. They wisely decided to regard the mental and religious education of the girls as of first importance, and those who followed these plans aimed to secure young women of intelligence from the surrounding towns, and stimulate them to seek improvement in their leisure hours.

Besides the free Grammar School there were innumerable night schools; and most of the churches provided, by means of "Social Circles," opportunities for improvement. So in Lowell there was a wide-awake set of girls working for their daily bread, with a true idea of the dignity of labor, and with the determination to make the most of themselves. They reasoned thus, as Miss Larcom expressed it: "That the manufacture of cloth should,

[1] *An Idyl of Work*, p. 34.

as a branch of feminine industry, ever have suffered a shadow of discredit, will doubtless appear to future generations a most ridiculous barbarism. To prepare the clothing of the world seems to have been regarded as womanly work in all ages. The spindle and the distaff, the picturesque accompaniments of many an ancient legend — of Penelope, of Lucretia, of the Fatal Sisters themselves — have, to be sure, changed somewhat in their modern adaptation to the machinery which robes the human millions; but they are, in effect, the same instruments, used to supply the same need, at whatever period of the world's history."

A few facts will show the character of these girls. One of the ministers was asked how many teachers he thought he could furnish from among the working-girls. He replied, "About five hundred." A lecturer in the Lowell Lyceum stated that four fifths of his audience were factory girls, that when he entered the hall most of the girls were reading from books, and when he began his lecture every one seemed to be taking notes. Charles Dickens, after his visit to Lowell in 1842, wrote: "I solemnly declare that from all the crowd I saw in the different factories, I cannot recall one face that gave me a painful impression; not one young girl whom, assuming it to be a matter of necessity that she should gain her daily bread by the labor of her hands, I would have removed if I had the power."

Mrs. Larcom kept a boarding-house for the operatives, and Lucy was thrown in close association with these strong young women. She had access to the little accumulation of books that one of them had made, — Maria Edgeworth's "Helen," Thomas à Kempis, Bunyan's "Holy War," Locke "On the Understanding," and "Paradise Lost." This formed good reading for a girl of ten.

Lucy's sister Emeline started in the boarding-house two or three little fortnightly papers, to which the girls contributed. Each ran a troubled existence of a few months, and then gave place to its successor, bearing a new name. "The Casket," for a time, held their jewels of thought; then "The Bouquet" gathered their full-blown ideas into a more pretentious collection. The most permanent of these literary productions was one that started with the intention of being very profound, — it was called "The Diving Bell." The significance of the name was carefully set forth in the first number: —

"Our Diving Bell shall deep descend,
And bring from the immortal mind
Thoughts that to improve us tend,
Of each variety and kind."

Lucy soon became a poetical contributor; and when the paper was read, and the guessing as to the author of each piece began — for they were anonymous — the other girls were soon able to tell her work by its music and thought. Among the yellow and worm-eaten pages of the once popular "Diving Bell," we find the following specimen of her earliest poetry: —

"I sit at my window and gaze
At the scenery lovely around,
On the water, the grass, and the trees,
And I hear the brook's murmuring sound.

"The bird warbles forth his soft lays,
And I smell the sweet fragrance of flowers,
I hear the low hum of the bees,
As they busily pass the long hours.

"These pleasures were given to man
To bring him more near to his God,
Then let me praise God all I can,
Until I am laid 'neath the sod."

From the interest excited by these little papers, the desire of the girls became strong for more dignified literary expression; and by the advice and assistance of the Rev. Abel C. Thomas, of the Universalist Church, the "Lowell Offering" was started in October, 1840, and the "Operative's Magazine" originated in the Literary Society of the First Congregational Church. These two magazines were united, in 1842, in the "Lowell Offering." The editors of the "Offering," Miss Hariett Farley and Miss Hariot Curtiss, factory girls, were women of superior culture and versatility, and made the magazine a unique experiment in our literature. In its pages were clever sketches of home life, humorous and pathetic tales, charming fairy stories, and poems. Its contributors, like the editors, were mill-girls. It was successful for five years, at one time having a subscription list as high as four thousand, which the girls tried to increase by traveling for it, as agents. This periodical attracted wide attention by reason of its unusual origin. Selections were made from it, and published in London, in 1849, called, "Mind Among the Spindles;" and a gentleman attending the literary lectures, in Paris, of Philarète Chasles, was surprised to hear one in which the significance and merit of the "Lowell Offering" was the sole theme. Our young author contributed to the "Offering," over the signatures "Rotha," or "L. L.," a number of poems and short prose articles, proving herself to be of sufficient ability to stand as a typical Lowell factory girl.

The principle of the interest of manufacturers in the lives of their operatives was illustrated in Lowell, though it was not carried out always as intelligently as it should have been. Children were allowed to work too young. Lucy began to change the bobbins on the spinning frames at eleven years of age, and the hours of work were sometimes from five in the morning to seven at night. But the day passed pleasantly for her, the bobbins having to be changed only every three quarters of an hour; and the interval between these periods of work was occupied by conversation with the girls in the same room, or by sitting in the window overlooking the river. On the sides of one of these windows she had pasted newspaper clippings, containing favorite poems, which she committed to memory when she sat in this "poet's corner."

During these years of mill-work she formed some of the ruling ideas of her life, those that we can see influencing her later thoughts, in her poetry and prose, and, best of all, her living. Her sympathy for honest industry, without any regard for its fictitious position in so-called "society," was developed by her acquaintance with those earnest girls who were struggling for their own support and education. Her capacity for friendship was continually tested; she opened her nature to the influence of the other lives around her.

The questions in relation to human life and its meaning became part of her deepest interests. In private conversations with her companions, in the meetings at the churches, and in her own meditations, these thoughts struggled for a hearing:—

> "Oh, what questionings
> Of fate, and freedom, and how evil came,
> And what death is, and what the life to come,—
> Passed to and fro among these girls!"[1]

The answers she gave were the truest. Her thought instinctively turned to the Invisible Power of the Universe, not solely as an explanation of things as they exist, or as a philosophical postulate, but as a Spirit whose presence could be felt in nature, in persons, and in her own heart. In other words, a love for God as a Being of Love began to take possession of her; it seized upon her at times like the rushing inspiration of the prophets; her trust was what is spoken of in theology as an experimental knowledge. Her early training by Puritan methods in the thought of a Sovereign Lord, deeply

[1] *An Idyl of Work*, p. 69.

affected her, yet she seems to have rediscovered God for herself, in the beauty that her poet's eye revealed to her — beauties of river and sea and sky, of flowers rejoicing in their color and perfume, and of human sympathies. Welling up in her own soul, she felt the waters troubled by the angel's touch, and was confident of God.

With this faith as a guide, the answers to other questions became plain. Life itself was a gift which must be used in His service; no evil thought or purpose should be allowed to enter and interfere with the soul's growth; duties were the natural outlets of the soul; through them the soul found its happiness. When she thought of death, there was only one logical way of looking at it: as a transition into a fuller life, where the immortal spirits of men could draw nearer to each other and to God. She seems never, from the very first, to have had any doubts as to what the end of life meant. There was always the portal ready to open into the richer Kingdom of Heaven.

The churches in Lowell stimulated her religious thought. At thirteen years of age, she stood up before her beloved minister, Dr. Amos Blanchard, and professed her belief in the Christian religion, and for many years found refreshment in the Sunday services. But as she grew older, she found many of the doctrines of Calvinistic Orthodoxy difficult for her to accept, and she regretted the step she had taken. The worship was not always helpful to her, especially the long prayer: —

"That long prayer
Was like a toilsome journey round the world,
By Cathay and the Mountains of the Moon,
To come at our own door-stone, where He stood
Waiting to speak to us, the Father dear,
Who is not far from any one of us." [1]

She admired the picturesque Episcopal church of St. Ann's, with its vine-wreathed stone walls, "an oasis amid the city's dust." The Church for which this venerable edifice stood was to be her final religious home, and in its stately services and sacred rites she was to find the spiritual nourishment of her later years.

She took an interest in the movements of politics, especially the question of slavery; she was an Abolitionist with the strongest feelings, from the first. She had some scruples about working on the cotton which was produced by slave labor: —

"When I have thought what soil the cotton plant
We weave is rooted in, what waters it —
The blood of souls in bondage — I have felt
That I was sinning against light, to stay
And turn the accursèd fibre into cloth
For human wearing. I have hailed one name —
You know it — 'Garrison' — as a soul might hail
His soul's deliverer." [2]

Whenever a petition for the abolition of slavery was circulated, to be sent to Congress, it was always sure to have the name of Lucy Larcom upon it. The poetry of Mr. Whittier had aroused her spirit, and though she does not seem to have written any of her stirring anti-slavery verses until

[1] *An Idyl of Work*, p. 74. [2] *Ibid*, p. 136.

years later, she was nursing the spark that during the Civil War blew into a flame.

It was in 1843, while in Lowell, that she first met Mr. Whittier, who was editing the "Middlesex Standard." Being present at one of the meetings of the "Improvement Circle," he heard her read one of her poems, "Sabbath Bells:" —

"List! a faint, a far-off chime!
'T is the knell of holy time,
Chiming from the city's spires,
From the hamlet's altar fires,
Waking woods and lonely dells,
Pleasant are the Sabbath bells."

This introduction began one of her most beautiful friendships; it lasted for half a century. She learned to know and love the poet's sweet, noble sister, Elizabeth, and Lucy was treated by her like a sister. There was something in Miss Larcom's nature not unlike Mr. Whittier's, — the same love for the unobserved beauties of country life, the same energy and fire, the same respect for the honest and sturdy elements in New England life, the same affection for the sea and mountains, and a similar deep religious sense of the nearness of God.

Having worked five years in the spinning-room, she was transferred at her own request to the position of book-keeper, in the cloth-room of the Lawrence Mills. Here, having more time to herself, she devoted to study the minutes not required by her work, reading extracts from the best books, and writing many of the poems that appeared in the "Offering."

It was her habit to carry a sort of prose sketch-book, not unlike an artist's, in which she would jot down in words the exact impression made upon her by a scene or a natural object, using both as models from which to draw pictures in words. In this way she would describe, for instance, an autumn leaf, accurately giving its shape, color, number of ribs and veins, ending with a reflection on the decay of beauty. In turning over the leaves of this sketch-book, one finds descriptions of the gnarled tree with its bare branches thrusting themselves forth in spiteful crookedness; the butterfly lying helpless in the dust with its green robes sprinkled with ashes; the wind in the pines singing a melancholy tune in the summer sunlight; and other subjects of equal beauty. As an illustration of these prose-poems, the suggestion for which she derived from Jean Paul Richter, the following may be of interest: it is called, "Flowers beneath Dead Leaves:"—

"Two friends were walking together beside a picturesque mill-stream. While they walked they talked of mortal life, its meaning and its end; and, as is almost inevitable with such themes, the current of their thoughts gradually lost its cheerful flow.

"'This is a miserable world,' said one. 'The black shroud of sorrow overhangs everything here.'

"'Not so,' replied the other. 'Sorrow is not a

shroud; it is only the covering Hope wraps about her when she sleeps.'

"Just then they entered an oak grove. It was early spring, and the trees were bare; but the last year's leaves lay thick as snowdrifts upon the ground.

"'The liverwort grows here, I think, — one of our earliest flowers,' said the last speaker. 'There, push away the leaves, and you will see it. How beautiful, with its delicate shades of pink, and purple and green, lying against the bare roots of the oak tree! But look deeper, or you will not find the flowers: they are under the dead leaves.'

"'Now I have learned a lesson which I shall not forget,' said her friend. 'This seems to me to be a bad world; and there is no denying that there are bad things in it. To a sweeping glance it will sometimes seem barren and desolate; but not one buried germ of life and beauty is lost to the All-Seeing Eye. Having the weakness of human vision, I must believe where I cannot see. Henceforth, when I am tempted to despair on account of evil, I will say to myself, Look deeper; look under the dead leaves, and you will find flowers.'"

Lucy Larcom almost imperceptibly slipped into womanhood during these Lowell years. From being an eager and precocious child, she became an intelligent and thoughtful woman. The one characteristic which seemed most fully defined was her tendency to express her thoughts in verse and prose. As is the case with young authors, her early verses were artificial, the sentiments were often borrowed, and the emotions were not always genuine. It is not natural to find a healthy young girl writing on such themes as "Earthly joys are fleeting," "Trust not the world, 't will cheat thee." "The murderer's request" was —

> "Bury me not where the breezes are sighing
> O'er those whom I loved in my innocent days."

But when she wrote out of her own experience, and recorded impressions she had felt, there was a touch of reality in her work that gave some prophecy of her future excellence. She could write understandingly about the boisterous March winds, or "school days," —

> "When I read old Peter Parley,
> Like a bookworm, through and through,
> Vainly shunned I Lindley Murray,
> And dull Colburn's 'Two and Two.'"

One cannot find any evidence that she made a study of verse-making, not even possessing "Walker's Rhyming Dictionary." Her powers were cultivated mainly by reading the poetry of others and unconsciously catching their spirit and metre. Her ear for music helped her more than her knowledge of tetrameters or hexameters.

The most important results of these years were the development of her self-reliance and sweetness, the stirring up of her ambitions to win an education, and the dawnings of her spiritual life. She was laying up stores of impressions and memories, also, that were to be permanently preserved in her more finished poems of later years. The imagery of her maturer verse recalls her early days, when in the freedom of childhood she roamed the fields and the woods, and lived on the banks of the Merrimac. We see her youth again through her reminiscences of the barberry cluster sweetened by the frost; the evening primrose; roses wet with briny spray; the woodbine clambering up the cliff; heaps of clover hay; breezes laden with some rare wood scent; the varied intonations of the wind; hieroglyphic lichens on the rocks; the mower whistling from the land; the white feet of the children pattering on the sand; the one aged tree on the mountain-top, wrestling with the storm wind; the candles lighted at sunset in the gambrel-roofed houses; the lightning glaring in the face of the drowning sailor; the tragedy of unconscious widowhood; the mill-wheel, the hidden power of the mill, with its great dripping spokes; and the mystery of meeting and blending horizons.

In the spring of 1846 the scene of Lucy Larcom's life was changed, when her sister Emeline married, and went to seek a home in the West, for she shared with the new family their pioneer life in Illinois. A few days before they started on their journey, she wrote some lines of farewell in her scribbling-book, which show that she was beginning to use real experiences for the subject of her verses.

"Farewell to thee, New England!
Thou mother, whose kind arm

Hath e'er been circled round me,
  The stern and yet the warm.
Farewell! thou little village,
  My birthplace and my home,
Along whose rocky border
  The morning surges come.
Thy name shall memory echo,
  As exiled shell its wave.
Art thou my home no longer?
  Still keep for me a grave."

CHAPTER II.

IN ILLINOIS.

1846–1852.

A JOURNEY from Massachusetts to Illinois, in 1846, was long, and filled with inconveniences. A little time-worn diary, written in pencil, kept by Lucy Larcom on the journey, is interesting for itself, and preserves the record of the difficulties that beset early travelers to the West.

Monday, April 13, 1846. Returned to Boston in the morning, and now, in the afternoon, we have really started. Passing through Massachusetts and Connecticut, we encountered a snowstorm, something quite unexpected at this season! Came on board the steamboat "Worcester," in darkness. And here we are, three of us, squeezed into the queerest little cubby-hole of a state-room that could be thought of. We all sat down on the floor and laughed till we cried, to see ourselves in such close companionship! We had a dispute, just for the fun of it, as to who should occupy the highest shelf. It was out of the question to put E. and the baby up there, and for myself, I painted the catastrophe which would occur, should I come down with my full weight upon the rest, in such glowing colors, that they were willing to consign me to the second shelf; and here I lie while the rest are asleep (if they can sleep on their first steamboat trip) trying to write of my wonderful experiences as a traveler.

Tuesday. Alas! Must I write it? The boast of our house must cease. When it has been said with so much pride that a Larcom was never seasick! — I have proved the contrary. I only thought to eat a bit of "'lasses gingerbread," on occasion of my departure from Yankee Land, and while I lay to-day in my berth, I was inwardly admonished that the angry Neptune was not pleased with my feasting, and I was obliged to yield up the precious morsel as a libation to him. Small sleep had I this night.

In the morning, S. and I rose long before daylight, and went out to peep at the sea by moonlight. It was strange and new to see the path of the great creature in the waters. After daylight most of the passengers came on deck. It was delightful sailing into New York by sunrise.

Passing through Hellgate, I was reminded of the worthy Dutch who went this way long ago, as Dick Knickerbocker records. Passed Blackwell's Island, — saw prisoners at work, — looked like pigs. Also passed the fort on Frog's Neck; small beauty in the great smoky city for me; an hour's stay and a breakfast at the hotel were enough. Took the cars across New Jersey. Don't like the appearance of this State at all. Reached Philadelphia about noon. Went immediately aboard the "Ohio" — a beautiful boat, and a lovely afternoon it was when we sailed down the Delaware. The city looked so pleasant with the sun shining on it, and the green waving trees about it, while the waves looked so smooth in their white fringes, that I could have jumped overboard for joy! Never shall I forget that afternoon. At evening, took the cars to — somewhere, on the Chesapeake Bay, and thence to Baltimore on another boat. Saw hedges, for the first time, in Maryland. Had an unpleasant sail in an unpleasant boat. Sister and S. wretchedly seasick; so was nearly everybody, but I redeemed my fame, dancing attendance from baby to the sick ones continually. The wind blew, the boat rocked, and the tide was against us. One poor little Irish woman, who was going with her baby to meet her husband, was terribly frightened. I tried to comfort her, but she said "she would pull every curl out of her old man's head, for sending for her and the baby." All the while, a queer-looking German couple were on deck; the man appeared as if intoxicated, first scolding and then kissing! The wind was cold, but the man shook his fists when one young lady asked the woman to come inside and get warm. She would cry when he scolded her, and "make up" again as soon as he was disposed to. Then they would promenade together very lovingly and very awkwardly.

Came into Baltimore between ten and eleven.

S. had her pocket picked on the way! Stopped at the National Hotel for the night, and left B. again in the morning, in the cars. Glad enough, too, for I hate cities, and B. worst of all. Rode through Maryland. A very delightful state, but slavery spoils it. Saw the first log-cabin; it was quite decent-looking, in comparison with the idea I had formed of it. Stopped at a station where there were three little negroes sitting on a bench, sunning themselves, and combing each other's wool meanwhile. They looked the picture of ignorance and happiness.

Were all day Thursday riding through the State of Maryland. Saw flowers and trees in blossom: delightful country, quite hilly, and well watered. Followed the course of the Potomac a long way, and at noon stopped at Harper's Ferry, a wild-looking place, though I think not so romantic as a place we passed just before it, where the waters curve in gentle flow from between two bold hills. Now saw the mountains around Cumberland. At Cumberland, were squeezed into a stage, to cross the Alleghenies. Oh, what misery did we not endure that night! Nine, and a baby, in the little stage! I tried to reconcile myself to my fate, but was so cross if anybody spoke to me! When we got out of the stage in the morning I felt more like a snake crawling from a heap of rocks than anything else. We stretched ourselves, and took breakfast, such as we could get, at a poor-looking tavern. Then into the stage again, and over the mountains to Brownsville; never imagined mountains could be so high, when we were riding on mountains all the time. Reached Brownsville about twelve, — a dingy place down among the hills. Took a little walk here. Embarked for Pittsburgh; was glad enough to stow myself away into a berth and rest. Did n't trouble the Monongahela with a glance after the boat started, for I was "used up." Found ourselves at Pittsburgh in the morning, a dirty city indeed. Everything black and smoky. Should think the sun would refuse to shine upon it.

Friday noon. Here we take another boat — the "Clipper" — the prettiest one I have seen yet. Splendidly furnished, neat, comfortable berths, and all we could ask for. The Ohio is a beautiful stream. I sit in my state-room with the door open, "taking notes." I am on the Ohio side; the banks are steep, — now and then we pass a little town. We have stopped at one, now; men and boys are looking down on us from a sand-bank far above our heads. Why the people chose a sand-bank, when they might have had a delightful situation almost anywhere, I wonder much! Oh, dear! nothing looks like home! but I must not think of that, now.

Saturday noon. We are passing through a delightful country. Peach-trees along the banks of the river, in full bloom, reflected in the water by sunrise, and surrounded by newly-leaved trees of every shade of green, — they were beautiful indeed. Have been perfectly charmed with the varied prospect. Hills stretching down to the margin of the river, covered with trees, and sunny little cottages nestled at their base, surrounded with every sort of fruit-tree, — old trees hanging over the river, their topmost boughs crowned with the dark green mistletoe. Think I should like to live here a *little* while. Sat on the deck this forenoon, and sang "Sweet Home," and "I would not live alway," with Mr. C. and S. Thunder-storm this afternoon; went on deck after tea to see the sunset — beautiful! Water still, and reflecting gold from motionless clouds. Went out again at dusk, and heard the frogs singing. It seemed a little like Saturday evening at home; but no! Passed North Bend before sunset. Beautiful place: large house, standing back from the road, half hid by trees; a small green hill near the house covered with young trees; and a fine orchard in bloom on another hill, near by. The river bends on the Ohio side.

21st. Stopped at St. Louis, about ten o'clock. Lay here till nearly dark, waiting for canal to be mended. Oppressively hot; could not sit still nor sleep. Going through the canal very slowly.

22d. Passed through the locks in the night. Morning, — found Illinois on the right. Dogwort looked sweet among the light green foliage. Stopped at Evansville in the afternoon, and took in a freight of mosquitoes. Cabin full. Retired early, to get out of their way.

23d. Played chess, forenoon. Came to the north of the bend about ten. Went on deck to see the meeting of the waters. Grand sight. Cairo, small town on the point, has been overflowed. So near my new home; begin to be homesick.

The new home was destined to be a log-cabin on Looking-Glass Prairie, St. Clair County, Illinois, with the broad rolling country all around, and a few houses in sight. This settlement was designated "Frogdom" by some of the residents.

The little family had to put up with great inconveniences, the house not even being plastered, and the furniture being of the most primitive kind. Soon after their arrival, they were all ill with malarial fever, commonly called "agey," but their spirits never flagged. Lucy somewhere speaks of herself as having a cheerful disposition; it helped her, at this time, to deal with the discomforts of the novel surroundings. Her sister refers to her, in a letter to Beverly, as "our merry young sister Lucy."

Some of the neighbors were not as comfortable as these new farmers. One of them, living not very far off, had for a home a hastily constructed shanty, with a bunk for a bed, and innumerable rat-holes to let the smoke out when he had a fire. Others were "right smart" folk from Pennsylvania. Her main object, however, was not to be a farmer, but to become a district-school teacher. She soon secured a position; and began the itinerant life of a teacher, spending a few months in many different places. She received her salary every three months. Once, when there was a little delay in the payment, she requested it. The forty dollars were paid with the remark that "it was a powerful lot of money for only three months' teaching."

The rough boys and untrained girls called forth all her patience, and the need of holding their attention forced her to adopt a straightforward method of expressing herself. Sometimes her experiences were ludicrous. One day, having to discipline a mischievous urchin, she put him on a stool near the fireplace, and then went on with the lessons, not noticing him very much. Looking to see what he was doing, she was surprised at his disappearance from the room. The question was, "Where has he gone?" It was answered by one of the scholars, "He's gone up the chimney." He had indeed crawled up the wide open fireplace, and, having thus escaped, was dancing a jig in front of the school-house.

Miss Larcom taught in many different places — Waterloo, Lebanon, Sugar Creek, Woodburn — and generally the rate of payment was fourteen dollars a month. Board and lodging cost her one dollar and twenty-five cents a week. She did her own washing and ironing. The frequent change of schools made her form attachments for the children that had to be quickly broken. Speaking of a farewell at one school, she said, "The children cried bitterly when I dismissed them, whether for joy or sorrow it is n't for me to say."

Her letters to Beverly were brimful of fun;

they give, in an easy style, a vivid account of the hardships of these log-cabin days. The two following letters were written to her sisters, Abby and Lydia.

TO MRS. ABBY O. HASKELL.

LOOKING-GLASS PRAIRIE, May 19, 1846.

DEAR SISTER ABBY, — I think it is your turn to have a letter now, so I 've just snuffed the candle, and got all my utensils about me, and am going to see how quickly I can write a good long one.

Well, for my convenience, I beg that you will borrow the wings of a dove, and come and sit down here by me. There, — don't you see what a nice little room we are in? To be sure, one side of it has not got any *side* to it, because the man could n't afford to lath and plaster it, but that patch curtain that Emeline has hung up makes it snug enough for summer time, and reminds us of the days of ancient tapestried halls, and all that. That door, where the curtain is, goes into the entry; and there, right opposite, is another one that goes into the parlor, but I shall not go in there with you, because there are n't any chairs in there; you might sit on Emeline's blue trunk, or Sarah's green one, though; but I 'm afraid you 'd go behind the sheet in the corner, and steal some of Emeline's milk that she 's saving to make butter of; and then, just as likely as not, you 'd want to know why that square piece of board was put on the bottom of the window, with the pitchfork stuck into it to keep it from falling;

of course, we should n't like to tell you that there 's a square of glass out, and I suppose you don't know about that great tom-cat's coming in, two nights, after we had all gone to bed, and making that awful caterwauling. So you had better stay here in the kitchen, and I 'll show you all the things; it won't take long. That door at the top of three steps leads upstairs; the little low one close to it is the closet door, — you need n't go prying in there, to see what we 've got to eat, for you 'll certainly bump your head if you do; pass by the parlor door and the curtain, and look out of that window on the front side of the house; if it was not so dark, you might see the beautiful flower-beds that Sarah has made, — a big diamond in the centre, with four triangles to match it. As true as I live, she has been making her initials right in the centre of the diamond! There 's a great S, and an M, but where 's the H? Oh! you don't know how that dog came in and scratched it all up, and laid down there to sun himself, the other day. We tell her there 's a sign to it, — losing her maiden name so soon. She declares she won't have it altered by a puppy, though. These two windows look (through the fence) over to our next neighbor's; that 's our new cooking-stove between them; is n't it a cunning one? the funnel goes up clear through Emeline's bedroom, till it gets to "outdoors." We keep our chimney in the parlor. Then that door on the other side looks away across the prairie, three or four miles; and that brings us to where we started from.

As to furniture, this is the table, where I am writing; it is a stained one, without leaves, large enough for six to eat from, and it cost just two dollars and a quarter. There are a half dozen chairs, black, with yellow figures, and this is the rocking-chair, where we get baby to sleep. That is E.'s rag mat before the stove, and George fixed that shelf for the water-pail in the corner. The coffee-mill is close to it, and that 's all. Now don't you call us rich? I 'm sure we feel grand enough.

Now, if you would only just come and make us a visit in earnest, Emeline would make you some nice corn-meal fritters, and you should have some cream and sugar on them; and I would make you some nice doughnuts, for I 've learned so much; and you should have milk or coffee, just as you pleased; it is genteel to drink coffee for breakfast, dinner, and supper, here. Then, if you did n't feel satisfied, we should say that it was because you had n't lived on johnny-cakes and milk a week, as we did.

I have got to begin to be very dignified, for I am going to begin to keep school next Monday, in a little log-cabin, all alone. One of the "committee men" took me to Lebanon, last Saturday, in his prairie wagon, to be examined. You 've no idea how frightened I was, but I answered all their questions, and did n't make any more mistakes than they did. They told me I made handsome figures, wrote a good hand, and spoke correctly, so I begin to feel as if I knew most as much as other folks.

Emeline does not gain any flesh, although she has grown very handsome since she came to the land of "hog and hominy." Your humble servant is as fat as a pig, as usual, though she has not tasted any of the porkers since her emigration, for the same reason that a certain gentleman would not eat any of Aunt Betsey's cucumbers, — "not fit to eat." That 's my opinion, and if you had seen such specimens of the living animal as I have, since I left home, you 'd say so, too. LUCY.

TO MRS. I. W. BAKER.

LOOKING-GLASS PRAIRIE, June 9, 1846.

DEAR SISTER, — Here I am, just got home from school; all at once a notion takes me that I want to write to you, and I 'm doing it. I 'm sitting in our parlor, or at least, what we call our parlor, because the cooking-stove is not in it, and because Emeline has laid her pretty rag mat before the hearth, and because the sofa is in here. There! you did n't think we 'd get a sofa out here, did you? Well, to be sure, it is n't exactly like your sofa, because it is n't stuffed, nor covered, nor has it any back, only the side of the house; nor any legs, only red ones, made of brick; dear me! I 'm afraid you 'll "find out," after all, — but it certainly did come all the way from St. Louis, in the wagon with the other furniture. We keep our "cheers" in the kitchen, and we find that Becky Wallis's definition of them, *i. e.*, "to sit on," don't tell the whole story now.

But don't you want to hear how we like it, out here, in this great country? Oh, happy as clams! and we have n't been homesick, either, only once in a while, when it seemed so queer getting "naturalized," that we could n't help "keepin' up a terrible thinkin'." By the way, we were all sick last week, — no, not all; Emeline and the baby were not. George and Sarah and I all had the doctor at once. I was taken first, and had the most violent attack, and got well soonest. Our complaint was remittent fever, which is only another name for chills and fever, I suspect. I felt ashamed to get "the chills" so soon after coming here, and I believe the doctor was kind enough to call it something else. I did have one regular "chill," though; the blood settled under my nails, and though I did n't shake, I shivered "like I had the agey." That 's our Western phraseology. Blue pills and quinine I thought would be the death of me; but I believe they cured me after all. I had to leave school for a week, but yesterday I commenced again.

My school! Oh, the times I do have there with the young Suckers! I have to walk rather more than a mile to it, and it is in just the most literal specimen of a log-cabin that you can form any idea of. 'T is built of unhewn logs, laid "criss-cross," as we used to say down in the lane; the chinks filled up with mud, except those which are not filled up "at all, at all," and the chimney is stuck on behind the house. The floor lies as easy as it can, on the ground, and the benches are, some of them (will you believe it?), very much like our sofa. They never had a school in this district before, and my "ideas" are beginning to "shoot" very naturally, most of them. I asked one new scholar yesterday how old she was. "Don't know," she said, "never was inside of a schoolhouse before." Another big girl got hold of my rubbers the other day, "Ouch," said she, "be them Ingin robbers? I never seen any 'fore." Some of them are bright enough to make up for all this, and on the whole I enjoy being "schoolma'am" very much. I have not seen a snake since I came here, and if I did n't have to pass through such a sprinkling of cattle on my way to school, I should n't have a morsel of trouble. Everybody turns his "cattle-brutes" out on the open prairie to feed, and they will get right into my path, and such a mooing and bellowing as they make! George has three big cows and two little ones, and two calves, and a horse, and ten hens, and a big pig and a little one: only the big pig has dug a subterranean passage, and "runned away." And I don't milk the cows, and I won't learn to, if I can help it, because they will be so impolite as to turn round and stare me in the face always when I go near them.

Talk to me about getting married and settling down here in the West! I don't do that thing till I 'm a greater goose than I am now, for love nor money. It is a common saying here, that "this is a fine country for men and dogs, but women and oxen have to take it." The secret of it is that farmers' wives have to do all their work in one room, without any help, and almost nothing to work with. If ever I had the mind to take the vestal vow, it has been since I "emigrated." You 'll see me coming back one of these years, a "right smart" old maid, my fat sides and cheeks shaking with "the agey," to the tune of "Oh, take your time, Miss Lucy!"

I 've a good mind to give you a picture, for the sun is setting, and it makes me feel "sort o' romantic." Well, in the first place, make a great wide daub of green, away off as far as the sunset; streak it a little deeper, half-way there, for the wheat fields. A little to the right make a smooth, bluish green hill, as even as a potato hill, — that 's the Blue Mound. A little one side, make a hundred little red, black, and white specks on the grass, — them 's the "cattle-brutes." Right against the sun, you may make a little bit of a house, with one side of the roof hanging over like an umbrella, — that 's Mr. Merritt's. And here, right before you, make a little whitewashed log-cabin, with a Virginia fence all round it ever so far, and a bank on one side sloping down to a little brook, where honey-locust trees a-plenty grow. Make it green in a great circle all round, just as if you were out at sea, where it 's all blue; then put on a great round blue sky for a cover, throw in a very few clouds, and have a "picter," or part of one, of our prairie. There now, don't you think I should have been an artist, if circumstances had only developed my natural genius? All send love. Your everlasting sister, LUCY.

The pioneer family found it necessary to move their main headquarters, for Mr. Spaulding, the husband of Emeline, decided to give up farming, and become a minister. Ministers were scarce in that region, and seeing the need, he carried out a cherished plan of his youth by being ordained as a preacher of the gospel. Consequently they deserted their home, and went to Woodburn, with all their newly acquired furniture on three wagons, each drawn by three yoke of oxen that splashed through the mud, until they came to a cottage possessing more rooms than the house they had left, though the doors were made of rough boards. These rooms were papered by Lucy, with Boston "Journals." She grew to love this cottage, for it represented home to her on the prairie.

In spite of cares and unpoetical methods of living, her pen was not idle. She wrote of the little prairie rose: —

"Flowers around are thick and bright,
The purple phlox and orchis white,
The orange lily, iris blue,
And painted cups of flaming hue.
Not one among them grows,
So lovely as the little prairie rose."

The spirit of a jolly ride over the snow she caught in some lines called "A Prairie Sleigh-Ride:" —

"Away o'er the prairies, the wide and the free,
Away o'er the glistening prairies with me;
The last glance of day lights a blush on the snow,
While away through the twilight our merry steeds go."

She also felt the awe inspired by the silence and immensity of the land, with the blue heavens arching over.

"But in its solemn silence,
Father, we feel thou art
Filling alike this boundless sea,
And every humble heart."

When Lucy had been teaching district school for two years, she was conscious of her deficiencies, and longed for a chance to acquire a more thorough education. She wished to fit herself for promotion in her calling, and ambitions to become a writer were not absent from her thoughts. An opportunity for study presented itself in Monticello Female Seminary, Alton, Illinois, which was about twenty miles away from her home. This institution, founded by Captain B. Godfrey, was one of the first established in the country for the higher education of women. The prospectus of 1845, adorned with a stiff engraving of the grounds and large stone building, offered in its antiquated language, attractions which seemed to suit her needs: "The design of the Institution, is to furnish Young Ladies with an education, *substantial*, *extensive* and *practical*,—that shall at the same time develop harmoniously their physical, intellectual, and moral powers, and prepare them for the sober realities and duties of life." All this was to be had for a sum less than one hundred dollars, in a situation so healthful that there "had never been a death in the institution."

TO MRS. I. W. BAKER.

WOODBURN, November 23, 1848.

. . . I have a new notion in my head, and I suppose I may as well broach it at once. There is a certain Seminary in the neighborhood at which I am very anxious to pass a year or so. It is one of the best of its kind. I want a better education than I have. Now I am only a tolerable sort of a "school-ma'am" for children; but if I could teach higher branches, I could make it more profitable, with less labor. I suppose I must call teaching my trade; and though I don't like it the "very best kind," I want to understand it as well as possible. And then if I don't always keep school I may be able to depend on my pen for a living. . . .

As Lucy was not able to pay the full tuition, the principal, Miss Fobes, arranged that she should be both student and teacher, thus helping to defray her expenses. She entered the school in September, 1849, and studied, in earnest, history, metaphysics, English literature, and higher mathematics, and laid the foundation for a thorough education.

Her schoolmates remember with pleasure the beauty of her life at Monticello. They speak of the gentleness and peculiar sweetness of her character. Nothing coarse or mean could be associated with her. Being older than the other girls she was looked up to with reverence by them. Her singular purity of mind was illustrated by a remark to one of her companions, when they were talking about the Christian life, — "I never knew there was any other way to live." One of her schoolmates writes: "I felt homesick, until one day I was introduced to a large, fair-faced woman, and looked up to meet a pair of happy blue eyes smiling down upon me, so full of sweet human kindness that the clouds fell straight away. And from that day the kindness never failed me — I think it never failed anyone. 'The sunshine of her face' were words that went out in many of my letters in those days."

She studied industriously each subject of the course. Her note-books contain full extracts from the authors she was reading, with long comments by herself. Those on philosophy indicate a mind naturally delighting in speculative questions; and when her reasoning touches upon theology, she seems especially in earnest. History appealed to her imagination, and she seized upon the more dramatic incidents for comment. English literature opened a new world of thought to her, and she studied enthusiastically the origin and growth of poetry. In these studies of English it was first suggested to her that there was an art of versification, which could be cultivated. From this time her lines conform more to poetic rules, her ear for music being supplemented by a knowledge of metre.

There was one subject she could not master, —

mathematics: "I am working on spherical trigonometry, just now. I don't fancy it much; it needs a clearer head than mine to take in such abstract matters as the sides and angles of the triangle that can be imagined, but not seen." She would exclaim, when studying Conic Sections, that she could see all the beauty, and feel all the poetry, but could not take the steps. When, however, after great work, she did understand a proposition, she accepted it as an eternal fact which God used for infinite purposes.

The girls at Monticello had a debating society. They gained confidence in speaking on such questions as, — "The blind man has more enjoyment in life, than the dumb man," or, "Does the development of science depend more upon genius than industry?" Youthful wits were sharpened as a result of affirming and denying these momentous propositions, in arguments as strong as could be had. Does not the following extract from one of Lucy's speeches present a typical picture of the fortunes of war in debate, when members are sometimes overcome by the weight of their own wisdom? "The member from Otter Creek arose and said that immigrants to this country were not the lowest classes, that they were quite a decent sort of people — but upon uttering these words, she was shaken by a qualm of conscience, or some sudden indisposition, and compelled to take her seat."

There were also compositions to be written. The

subjects assigned for these monthly tests of literary ability were as artificial as those for debate. The object of the teacher in our early schools seems to have been the selection of topics for essays as far removed from anything usual or commonplace as possible. One can very easily imagine what would be the style of an essay on the topic, "It is the high prerogative of the heroic soul to propagate its own likeness." Lucy managed to get a little humor into the discussion of the question, — "Was the building of Bunker Hill Monument a wise expenditure of funds?" She argued: "Is there a use in monuments? Perhaps not, literally. We have heard of no process by which Bunker Hill Monument might be converted into a lodging-house, and though we are aware that our thrifty brethren of Yankee-land have made it yield its quota of dollars and cents, so that any aspirant may step into a basket and be swung to the pinnacle of a nation's glory for ninepence, we are not in the habit of considering this its sole productive principle, unless gratitude and patriotism are omitted."

Miss Larcom remained at Monticello Seminary until her graduation in June, 1852. Miss Fobes says: "When she left the institution, with her diploma, and the benediction of her Alma Mater, we felt sure that, with her noble equipment for service, the result should be success in whatever field she should find her work." Her improvement had been so great that it was noticeable to the members of the family, who referred to her as "our learned sister."

TO MRS. ABBY O. HASKELL.

MONTICELLO SEMINARY, May 14th, 1850.

. . . But pray don't call me your "learned sister" any more; for if I deserved the title, it would make me feel like a something on a pedestal, and not plain Lucy Larcom: the sister of some half-dozen worthy matrons.

I think it must be a mistake about my having improved so *very* much; though I should be sorry to have lived all these years and made no advancement. Folks tell me that I am dignified, sometimes, but I don't know what it means. I have never tried to be, and I seem just as natural to myself as anything.

I don't know how I could ever get along with all your cares. I should like tending the babies well enough, but when it came to washing, baking, brewing, and mending, my patience would take "French leave." Still I don't believe that any married woman's trials are much worse than a "schoolma'am's." . . .

There was an event in her life in the West to be touched on. It relates to her one serious love affair. A deep attachment sprang up between Lucy and a young man who had accompanied her sister's family to Illinois, and for a time lived with them during their log-cabin experiences, but afterwards went to California. When he left, though they could hardly be called engaged, there was an understanding between them that, when he returned during the last days of her school life, they were to decide the matter finally. After three years of separation, they were no nearer a conclusion. Some years after this, it became clear to Miss Larcom that their marriage would not be for the best interests of either.

In 1852, her thoughts turned again to her native town of Beverly. Equipped with her Monticello education, she felt prepared to support herself by teaching in her congenial home in the East. The memories of her childhood drew her back in thought to her old home. She wrote to her brother Benjamin in March, "The almanac says I am twenty-eight years old, but really, Ben, I do believe it fibs, for I don't feel half so old. It seems only the other day that Lydia and I were sitting by the big kitchen fireplace, down the lane, and you opposite us, puffing cigar-smoke into our hair, and singing, 'My name is Apollyon.'"

To her sister Lydia, whose birthday was on the same day of the month as her own, she sent some verses recalling her childhood.

"In childhood we looked gayly out,
To see this blustering dawn begin
And hailed the wind whose noisy shout
Our mutual birthday ushered in.

"For cakes, beneath our pillow rolled,
We laughing searched, and wondered, too,
How mother had so well foretold
What fairy people meant to do."

CHAPTER III.

LIFE AT NORTON.

1853–1859.

In the autumn of 1853, Miss Larcom, having returned to Beverly, lived for a year with her sister, Mrs. Baker, in the pretty old-fashioned house on Cabot Street. Securing a few rooms in an unoccupied house not far away, she fitted them up as schoolroom and studio. Here she taught a little school with ten scholars. Most of these young girls were as far advanced as the second class at Monticello, and having already been instructed in the fundamental studies, they were not so difficult to teach as her untrained pupils in the West. The impression she made upon each of these young lives was strong, for, as a little family, she not only taught them the lessons, but gave them generously from her enthusiasm and faith. She imparted to them her love for all things true and beautiful. When the school year closed, she asked each girl to choose her favorite flower, upon which she wrote a few lines of verse, — on the hyacinth, signifying jealousy, — on the lily of the valley, meaning innocence.

"The fragrance Sarah would inhale
Is the lily of the vale:
'Humility,' it whispers low;
Ah! let that gentle breathing flow
Deep within, and then will you
Be a lily of the valley too."

One of these pupils wrote to her years after: "Among the teachers of my girlhood, you are the one who stands out as my model of womanhood."

While teaching, she still considered herself a scholar. Nor did she ever in after life overcome this feeling, for she was always eager to learn. When she was imparting her best instruction, and writing her most noteworthy books, she studied with great fidelity. At this time she took lessons in French and drawing; her love for color and form was always great. Often she had attempted in crude ways to preserve the spirit of a landscape, and so reproduce the color of the green ferns and variegated flowers; but now she set about the task in earnest. She had no special talent for painting, so she did nothing worthy of special notice, but some water-color sketches of autumn leaves, the goldenrod's "rooted sunshine," woodland violets, and the coral of the barberry, and apple-blossoms, "flakes of fragrance drifting everywhere," are very pretty. This study of painting, however, trained her observation, and prepared her to appreciate works of art by giving her some knowledge of the use of the palette. This early attempt at artist's work strengthened her love for pictures; and it was a special treat to her to visit the different galleries in Boston, where she was sure to be one of the first to see a celebrated painting.

It was a pleasure to her to be once more with her family, for the members of which she had the deepest affection. Writing to Miss Fobes, she expressed herself thus: "I am glad I came home, for I never realized before what a treasure my family circle was, nor how much I loved them. Then why do I not wish to stay? Simply because it does not seem to me that I can here develop the utmost that is in me. Ought I to be contented while that feeling remains?"

The feeling that she must develop "the utmost that is in me," impelled her through life, as a duty that she must regard. She was not without opportunities for cultivation in Beverly. There were the two weekly Lyceum lectures, with good speakers — Miss Lucy Stone had advocated woman's rights so ably that "even in this conservative town many became converts." However, she longed for a larger work, and was ready to accept the call to be a teacher in Wheaton Seminary, Norton, Massachusetts.

In the early winter of 1854, she began her work at Wheaton Seminary, the large school for girls, founded through the generosity of Judge Wheaton, in memory of his daughter. The subjects given her to teach were history, moral philosophy, literature, and rhetoric, including the duty of overlooking the greater part of the compositions.

Her spirit on entering upon this new work, is indicated by this letter: —

TO MISS P. FOBES.

WHEATON SEMINARY, NORTON, MASS.,
January 10, 1855.

DEAR MISS FOBES: — When I look back upon my life I think I see it divided into epochs similar to geological ages, when, by slow or sudden upheavings, I have found myself the wondering possessor of a new life in a new world. My years at Monticello formed such an epoch, and it is no flattery to say that to you I owe much of the richness and beauty of the landscape over which I now exult. For your teaching gave me intellectually a broader scope and firmer footing than I ever had ventured upon.

I know that I have done almost nothing as yet to show that I have received so much good. Life here seems to me not much more than "a getting ready to do." But in the consciousness of what it is to be a human being, created in the image of the divine, — in the gradual developing of new inner powers like unfolding wings, — in the joy of entering into the secrets of beauty in God's universe, — in the hopefulness of constant struggling and aspiring, I am rich.

I have been in this place only a few weeks and suppose the length of my stay will depend upon the satisfaction I give and receive. It is a pleasant school. Yours truly, LUCY LARCOM.

The length of her stay in Norton extended over eight important years of her life, from 1854 to 1862. These years were full of intellectual and religious struggles, of hard student life, of sweet companionships, of the beginnings of literary success, and of deep friendships. Earnestness and sincerity here became her characteristic traits; while her gentleness and patience, though sorely tried at times by the misconduct or failure of her scholars, became habitual with her.

One cannot think of the quiet life she led under the Norton elms, without picturing the tall graceful woman with her sweet face, low broad forehead, and soft blue eyes, moving about among the girls as a continual inspiration, always leading them by her presence and words into some region of sentiment, or beauty, or religion. In the schoolroom, ever dignified, she spoke in a low voice with the emphasis of real interest. In her own room, with its green carpet and white curtains, where she liked to retire for thought and work, surrounded by her books, a few pictures, and shells and pressed seaweed, she would prepare her lectures, and write her letters to her friends. There were sure to be flowers on her table, sent either by some loving scholar, or plucked by her own hand, — "I have some pretty things in my room; and flowers, so alive! As I look into their deep cups, I am filled with the harmonies of color and form. How warm a bright rose-pink carnation makes the room on a wintry day!" A scholar tells how, venturing into this retreat, she saw Miss Larcom quietly sitting in a rocking-chair, knitting stockings for the soldiers, during the War.

She was a conscientious student in preparing her lessons; she read the best books she could find in the school library, or could borrow from her friends. The notes of her lectures show great labor by their exhaustiveness. As a teacher, some of her power was derived from the clearness with which she presented the theme, and her picturesque style of expression. She invested the most lifeless topics with interest by the use of original and appropriate illustrations, — as will be seen in the following passage from a lecture on Anglo-Saxon poetry, in which she describes the minstrels: —

"The minstrels would sing, and the people would listen; and if the monks had listened too, they would sometimes have heard the irregularities of their lives chanted for the derision of the populace. For the bards assumed perfect independence in their choice of themes; liberty of the lyre seems to have been what liberty of the press is in these days. We can imagine the excitement in some quaint village, when the harp of one of these strollers was heard; how men and women would leave their work, and listen to these ballads. Those who have seen the magnetic effect of a hand-organ on village children, may have some idea of it; if the organ-grinder were also a famous story-teller, the effect would be greater. And this is something like what these ballad singers were to our elder brethren of Angle-land, in the childhood of civilization."

What excellent advice this is to girls, on the subject of their compositions, — "Get rid, if you can, of that formal idea of a composition to write, that stalks like a ghost through your holiday hours. Interest yourself in something, and just say your simple say about it. One mistake with beginners in writing is, that they think it important to spin out something long. It is a great deal better not to write more than a page or two, unless you have something to say, and can write it correctly."

The recitations in her class-room were of an unconventional character. Dealing with topics in the largest and most interesting way, she often used up the time in discussion, so that the girls who did not know their lessons sometimes took advantage of this peculiarity by asking questions, for the sole purpose of needlessly prolonging her explanation. It was often a joke among the scholars that she did not know where the lesson was; but so soon as she found the place, she made clear the portion assigned, and brought all her knowledge to bear so fully on the subject, that the scholars caught glimpses of unexplored fields of thought, which were made to contribute something to illustrate the theme in hand.

She did more for the girls than by simply teaching them in the class-room. She enlarged their intellectual life by founding a paper, called "The Rushlight," by which they not only gained confidence, but centralized the literary ability of the school. She explained the origin of the paper thus: "I said to myself, as I glanced over the bright things from the pile of compositions that rose before me semi-weekly, 'Why cannot we have a paper?' I said it to the girls, and to the teachers also, and everybody was pleased with the idea." She also founded the Psyche Literary Society, to stimulate the girls' studies in literature and art.

Another element in her power as a teacher was her personal interest in the girls. It was not solely an intellectual or literary interest, but she thought of their characters and religious training. To one of the girls she wrote, "I never felt it an interruption for you to come into my room; how we used to talk about everything!" When they were in trouble, they came naturally to her with their confidences. She was sometimes called "Mother Larcom," and she earned the title, for she acted like a mother to the homesick girl, and quieted by her gentle persuasiveness the tears of repentance, or bitter weeping of sorrow, of some of the more unfortunate of her pupils. Writing about one of the girls whose religious development she had watched, she said, "She is unfolding from the heart to God most openly, now. I am sure there is a deep life opening in her. I have rejoiced over her."

She discovered, through their moods — as in the case of one who was crying a great deal — or by the frequency of a permitted correspondence, their real or fancied love-affairs. After winning their confidence she could wisely advise them. Thus in one instance she wrote: "If such intimacy is true friendship, it will be a benefit to both; yet it is not without danger. I have seen the severest sufferings from the struggle between duty and feeling in such relations. I have seen life embittered by reason of the liberty allowed to a cousinly love, left unwatched. It is hard to keep the affections right in quantity and quality. But I need not say that a true love needs no limits; it is only falsehood that embitters every sweet and pure cup."

When the girls left school, they carried her love with them; and by correspondence and visits to their homes, where she was always a welcome guest, she followed them through the deepest experiences of their lives. One of her scholars said, "If I were to sum up the strong impression she made upon me, I should say it all in 'I loved her.'" Another wrote, "Miss Larcom was to me a peerless star, unattainable in the excellence and purity of her character. She stood as the ideal woman, whom I wished to be like."

When death invaded a home, she knew how to write: —

NORTON, October 7, 1855.

. . . Why is it we dread the brief parting of death so much? Do we really doubt meeting them again? Will they have lost themselves in the great crowd of immortals, so that when our time comes to follow them we cannot find them? I am just reading for the first time, "In Memoriam," and it fills my mind with these questions. I think I should be homesick in a mansion filled with angels, if my own precious friends whom I loved were not within call. . . .

The following letter shows her intimacy with the girls: —

TO MISS SUSAN HAYES WARD.

NORTON, April 2, 1855.

MY DEAR SUSIE, — I find it almost impossible to feel at home in a boarding-school; and then I know I never was made for a teacher, — a schoolmistress I mean. Still, among so many, one feels an inspiration in trying to do what is to be done, though the feeling that others would do it better is a drawback. And then, at such a place, I always find somebody to remember forever. For that I am thankful for my winter's experience. There are buds opening in the great human garden, which are not to be found at our own hearthstone: and it is a blessed task to watch them unfolding, and shield them from blight. And yet what can one mortal do for another? There is no such thing as helping, or blessing, except by becoming a medium for the divine light, and that is blessedness in itself.

It seems to me that to be a Christian is just to look up to God, and be blessed by his love, and then move through the world quietly, radiating as we go. . . .

The development of her own religious life was marked by many radical changes. She was no longer satisfied by the theology in which she had been reared. She sought new foundations for her belief. Her classes in philosophy led her into the world of controversy. Plato was constantly by her side, and she refreshed herself by reading Coleridge's "Aids to Reflection," from which she gained more nutriment than from any other religious book, except the Bible. Swedenborg taught her that "to grow old in heaven is to grow young." Sears's "Foregleams and Foreshadows" made her feel the joy of living, as presented in the chapter on "Home." She also read "Tauler's Sermons," and Hare's "Mission of the Comforter."

Interwoven with her religious thought were the life and influence of one of the dearest friends she ever knew, Miss Esther S. Humiston of Waterbury, Connecticut, a woman of rare powers, and wonderful sweetness of character. The two women were not unlike. They had the same spiritual longings, similiar views of life, and equal intellectual attainments. Miss Larcom looked up to Esther for guidance, and such was the perfect accord between them, that she wrote to her fully about her deepest thoughts, and most sacred experiences.

In the spring of 1858, she wrote thus to Esther: —
"You do not realize how very unorthodox I am. I do not think a bond of church-membership ought to be based upon intellectual belief at all, but that it should simply be a union in the divine love and

life. Now I do not formally belong to any particular church, — that is, I have a letter from a little Congregational church on the prairies, which I have never used, and I know not how, honestly, I can. For should I not be required virtually to say I believe certain things? I believe the Bible, but not just as any church I know explains it, and so I think I must keep aloof until I can find some band, united simply as Christian, without any "ism" attached. We all do belong to Christ's Church who love Him, so I do not feel lost or a wanderer, even though I cannot externally satisfy others."

TO ESTHER S. HUMISTON.

BEVERLY, MASS., August 2d, 1858.

. . . I regard Christianity as having to do with the heart and life, and not with the opinions; and my own opinions are not definite on many points. The disputed doctrines of total depravity, predestination, etc., with some of those distinctly called "evangelical," such as the atonement, and the duration of suffering after death, I find more and more difficulty in thinking about; so that I cannot yet say what "views" I "hold." There, — will you be my "sister confessor"? As I see things now, the "atonement" is to me, literally, the "at-onement," — our fallen natures lifted from the earthly by redeeming love, and brought into harmony with God; Jesus, the Mediator, is doing it now, in every heart that receives Him, and I think our faith should look up to Him as He is, the living

Redeemer, and not merely back to the dead Christ, — for "He is not dead." Then, as to the future state of those who die unrepentant: after probing my heart, I find that it utterly refuses to believe that there is any corner in God's universe where "hope never comes." There must be suffering, anguish, for those who choose sin, so long as they choose it; but can a soul, made in the image of God, who is Light, choose darkness forever? There is but one God, whose is the "kingdom, the power, and the glory, forever and ever;" is there any depth of darkness, which this sovereign radiance shall not at last pierce? I know the Bible testimony, and it seems to me that the inmost meaning, even of those fearfully denunciatory passages, would confirm this truth. Now, you can imagine how these sentiments would be received by an Orthodox Church. . . .

TO THE SAME.

NORTON, September 2, 1860.

. . . I enjoyed being with my friends. I told you that they were Universalists, but theirs is a better-toned piety than that of some Orthodox friends. Still, there was a want in it, a something that left me longing; it was as if they were looking at the sunlit side of a mountain, and never thought of the shadows which must be beyond. The mystery of life is in its shadows, and its beauty, in great part, too. There is n't shadow enough in Universalism to make a comprehensible belief for me.

And yet I believe there is no corner of God's universe where His love is not brooding, and seeking to penetrate the darkest abyss. . . .

The question about her marriage was definitely settled while she was at Norton. She decided, in the first place, on general grounds, that it would be best for her not to marry. There were various reasons for this. She had many premonitions of the breaking down of her health, which finally came in 1862, when she had to give up teaching; and owing to some exaggeration of her symptoms — for at times she felt that her mind might give way — she thought it unwise for her to take up the responsibilities of matrimony. In addition to this, she grew fond of her independence, and as her ability asserted itself, she seemed to see before her a career as an authoress, which she felt it her duty to pursue. Special reasons, of course, one cannot go into fully, though there are some features of them that may be mentioned; to Esther she stated an abundantly sufficient one, — "I am almost sure there are chambers in my heart that he could not unlock." She also differed radically from her lover on the subject of slavery. Her feelings as an abolitionist were so strong that she knew where there was such a division of sentiments a household could not be at peace within itself. This difference of opinion concerning all the questions that culminated in the Civil War resulted in a final refusal, which afterwards found public expression in her noted poem, "A Loyal Woman's No," an energetic refusal of a loyal woman to a lover who upheld slavery: —

"Not yours, — because you are not man enough
To grasp your country's measure of a man,
If such as you, when Freedom's ways are rough,
Cannot walk in them, — learn that women can!"

The poem was not written entirely out of her own experience. In making a confession about it to a friend, she says, "I have had a thousand tremblings about its going into print, because I feel that some others might feel hurt by the part that is not from my own experience. If it is better for the cause, let me and those old associations be sacrificed." The publication of the poem was justified by the way it was received everywhere. It was quoted in the newspapers all over the North. An answer was printed in "The Courier," called "A Young Man's Reply." This interested Miss Larcom, and she referred to it as "quite satisfactory, inasmuch as it shows that somebody whom the coat fitted put it on! If it does make unmanly and disloyal men wince, I am glad I wrote it."

TO ESTHER S. HUMISTON.

NORTON, June 1, 1858.

. . . I shall probably never marry. I can see reasons why it would be unwise for me; and yet I will freely tell you that I believe I should have been very happy, "if it might have been." A true marriage (*the* is the word I should have used) is the highest state of earthly happiness, — the flowing of the deepest life of the soul into a kindred soul, two spirits made one, — to be a double light and blessing to other souls has, I doubt not, been sometimes, though seldom, realized on earth. . . .

This touch of real romance in her life shows that she had a woman's true nature, and that she did not escape the gentle grasping of the divine passion, though she shook herself free from it, deciding that it was better for her to walk alone. Some lines of her poem, "Unwedded," suggest the reasons for her decision: —

"And here is a woman who understood
Herself, her work, and God's will with her,
To gather and scatter His sheaves of good,
And was meekly thankful, though men demur.

"Would she have walked more nobly, think,
With a man beside her, to point the way,
Hand joining hand in the marriage link?
Possibly, Yes: it is likelier, Nay."

TO MISS ESTHER S. HUMISTON.

NORTON, January 15, 1859.

. . . The books came through the post-office, with the note separate; they were brought to me while I was having a class recite logic in my room, — the dryest and most distasteful of all subjects to me, but it is a select class, and that makes up for the study. The young ladies who compose it are on quite familiar terms with me, and when the messenger said, "Three books and two letters for

Miss Larcom," their curiosity was greatly excited, and there was so much sly peeping at corners and picking at strings that they were not, on the whole, very *logical*. They asked to hold them for me till I was ready to open them, and I believe in letting "young ladies" act like children while they can. . . . I was thinking how much I should enjoy a quiet forenoon writing to you, when the words, "Study hour out" — accompanied the clang of the bell, and a Babel of voices broke into the hall outside my door.

I am trying not to hear — to get back into the quiet places of thought where your letters, open before me, were leading me, but I cannot; there is a jar, a discord, — and I suppose it is selfish in me not to be willing to be thus disturbed. How I long for a quiet place to live in! I never found a place still enough yet. But all kinds of natural sounds, as winds, waters, and even the crying of a baby, if not *too* loud and protracted, are not noises to me. Is it right to feel the sound of human voices a great annoyance? One who loved everybody would always enjoy the "music of speech," I suppose, and would find music where I hear only discord.

TO THE SAME.

Sabbath evening.

. . . I read in school yesterday morning, something from the "Sympathy of Christ." We have had some very naughty girls here, and have had to think of expulsion; but one of them ran away, and so saved us the trouble. How hard it is to judge the erring rightly — Christianly. I am always inclined to be too severe, for the sake of the rest; one corrupt heart that loves to roll its corruption about does so much evil. I do not think that a school like this is the place for evil natures — the family is the place, it seems to me, or even something more solitary. And yet there have been such reforms here, that sometimes I am in doubt. When there is a Christian, sympathizing heart to take the erring home, and care for her as a mother would, that is well. But we are all so busy here, with the *everythings*. I am convinced that I have too much head-employment altogether; I get hardly breathing time for heart and home life. . . .

In 1854, Miss Larcom published her first book, — "Similitudes from the Ocean and the Prairie." It was a little volume of not more than one hundred pages, containing brief prose parables drawn from nature, with the purpose of illustrating some moral truth. The titles of the Similitudes suggest their meaning: "The Song before the Storm;" "The Veiled Star;" "The Wasted Flower;" and "The Lost Gem." Though the conception was somewhat crude, yet her desire to find in all things a message of a higher life and a greater beauty, showed the serious beginnings of the poet's insight, which in after years was to reveal to her so many hidden truths. She characterized the book as "a very immature affair, often entirely childish."

Her first distinct literary success was the writing of the Kansas Prize Song, in 1855. When Kansas was being settled, the New England Emigrant Aid Company offered a prize of fifty dollars for the best song, written with the object of inspiring in the emigrants the sentiments of freedom. The power of a popular melody was to be used in maintaining a free soil. She gained this prize; and her stirring words were sung all through the West. They were printed, with the appropriate music of Mr. E. Norman, on cotton handkerchiefs, which were given away by the thousand.

> "Yeomen strong, hither throng,
> Nature's honest men;
> We will make the wilderness
> Bud and bloom again;
> Bring the sickle, speed the plough,
> Turn the ready soil;
> Freedom is the noblest pay
> For a true man's toil.
>
> "Ho, brothers! come, brothers!
> Hasten all with me;
> We 'll sing upon the Kansas plains
> A song of liberty."

Her next little book, "Lottie's Thought-book," was published by the American Sunday School Union, Philadelphia, in 1858. Not unlike the Similitudes in its method of teaching by parables, it gave the thoughts of a clever child, as they would be suggested by such scenes as a beautiful spring morning in the country, "when glad thoughts praise God;" the first snow, typifying the purity of the earth; or the thought of the joy of living, in the chapter "Glad to be alive" that recalls an exclamation she uses in one of her letters, "Oh! how happy I am, that I did not die in childhood!" These little books are like the inner biography of her youth, a pure crystal stream of love, reflecting the sunlight in every ripple and eddy.

She also wrote for various magazines, notably "The Crayon," in which appeared some criticisms of poetry, especially Miss Muloch's, and some of her poems, like "Chriemhild," a legend of Norse romance. The only payment she received was the subscription to the magazine. Her famous poem, "Hannah Binding Shoes," was first printed in the "Knickerbocker," without her knowledge, — then a few months later, in "The Crayon." This fact gave rise to the accusation of plagiarism which, though it greatly annoyed her, brought her poem into general notice. Having sent the poem to the "Knickerbocker," but not receiving any answer about its acceptance, she concluded that it had been rejected. She then sent it to "The Crayon," where it appeared, but in the mean time it had been printed in the "Knickerbocker." The editor of the last-named paper wrote a letter to the "New York Tribune," in which he accused Lucy Larcom of being "a literary thiefess," and claimed the "stolen goods." In answer to this, Miss Larcom wrote immediately a reply to the "Tribune."

NORTON, MASS., February 13, 1858.

TO THE EDITOR OF THE NEW YORK TRIBUNE:

SIR, — Will you please say to "Old Nick" that he does not tell the truth. His statements regarding me, in your paper, February 10, are not correct. Lucy Larcom is not a "literary thiefess;" "Hannah Binding Shoes" was not written "five or six years," but about four years since. I have only to blush that I wrote it, and that I sent it to the editor of the "Knickerbocker."

The latter was done at a time when it seemed desirable for me to attempt writing for pecuniary profit, — a very ridiculous idea, of course, — and I enclosed the poem in a letter, intimating such a desire to that gentleman, and supposing that courtesy would suggest that the letter should be answered, or the poem returned. As neither of these things was done, I innocently considered it my own property, and sent it to "The Crayon," as an original composition.

I hereby reclaim from "Old Nick," my "stolen goods," which he has inadvertently advertised.

Yours truly, LUCY LARCOM.

She wrote rather a severe letter to the "most honorable Old Nick" himself, in which she says, "In my ignorance, I supposed that editors were as polite as other people, in such matters as answering letters, and acknowledging even small favors. I am sure I never would have sent you a poem, if I had supposed you would one day have accused me of stealing it, and I hereby promise with sincere penitence, never to do so again. I suppose I can hardly look for the courtesy of an explanation as public as your accusation has been."

She also wrote an explanation to Mr. John Durand, the editor of "The Crayon."

TO JOHN DURAND.

NORTON, February 12, 1858.

DEAR MR. DURAND, — "Hannah Binding Shoes" I may truly say is "a poor thing, sir, but mine own." I should hardly have supposed that the identity of so humble an individual would be thought worth calling in question. The poem was written four years since, and was sent to the editor of the "Knickerbocker" in my own name, but as I received no acknowledgment from him, and have never seen a copy of the paper since, I supposed it either failed to reach him, or was not accepted. Was I not justifiable in sending it to you? I had no idea that it had been published before.

Yours truly, LUCY LARCOM.

"Hannah Binding Shoes" was set to music, and became very popular. Rev. Samuel Longfellow wrote her, "I wish you could have heard, as I did the other evening, 'Hannah' sung by Adelaide Phillips." Together with its sequel, "Skipper Ben," it recalled an incident very common in a New England sea-town, where ships were lost and lovers never returned, where every home had in it hearts that beat for those out at sea, and where women stood on the shore and strained their eyes looking for a sail. In these verses, as in all her poetry of the sea, she has caught the dirge in the wind, and the lonesome sound of beating waves when the skipper "faced his fate in a furious night."

In 1859 Miss Larcom tried, at the suggestion of many friends, to find a publisher for a volume of verses, but she was unsuccessful. A letter from Mr. Whittier accompanying the manuscript did not win Ticknor and Fields to her side. She took a very sensible view of her discomfiture.

TO JOHN DURAND.

NORTON, October 29, 1860.

. . . I should have regarded the thought of publishing as premature; but most of my friends are not artistic, and do not look upon my unripe fruits as I do. What I have written is at least genuine, sincere. I believe it is in me to do better things than I have done, and I shall work on in the faith of leaving something that will find its true place in the right time, because of the life there is in it. To live out, to express in some way the best there is in us, seems to me to be about all of life. . . .

After Miss Larcom's return from the West, the friendship with the Whittiers ripened and became a factor in her life. The gentle sweetness of the poet's sister Elizabeth soon won its way to her heart, and the strength of the man greatly impressed her. They grew very fond of her, and took an interest in her literary work. The attachment that Elizabeth formed for her was based on a most genuine love. In one of her letters she wrote, "Dear, dear Lucy, — Let me thank thee for all thy love. I can never tell thee how sweet it has been to me. I could have cried to think of thy loving care for me." Again: — "I wish I could see thee oftener. I need thee. I feel a little more rest with thee than with most. Thou hast done me good since I first knew thee." The two lives mingled and blended in the contact of companionship, for refinement of feeling, delicacy of thought, and strength of moral purpose, were characteristic of both. Mr. Whittier found her companionable, and admired her sincerity and poetical ability, which he recognized very early. It was one of Miss Larcom's greatest pleasures, while at Norton, to run off and spend a few days at Amesbury in the household that she loved. What Mr. Whittier said, she knew to be true, — "Thee will always find the latchstring out;" and when away, she knew she was remembered, for Elizabeth sent her word that "Greenleaf has just filled thy blue and gold vase with the yellowest of flowers."

Here is a letter to her, from Mr. Whittier, as early as 1853.

September 3, 1853.

My Dear Friend, — I thank thee for thy note. The personal allusion would be flattering enough, did I not know that it originated in a sad misconception and overestimate of one who knows himself to be "no better than he should be." It is a way we have. We are continually investing somebody or other with whatever is best in ourselves. It does not follow that the objects themselves are worth much. The vines of our fancy often drape the ugliest stumps in the whole forest.

I am anxious to see thy little book in print.[1] Whatever may be its fate with the public at large, I feel quite sure it will give thee a place in the best minds and hearts. The best kind of fame, after all. Thy friend, J. G. WHITTIER.

At Mr. Whittier's suggestion, she used to submit her work to him for criticism; and he always indicated what he considered faulty, in rhyme or metre. This practical training in the art of verse-making was valuable to her. She continued it for many years until she felt that she ought to be more self-reliant. Then she printed without consulting him, and, at first, he reproved her for it. "But," she said, "you have taught me all that I ought to ask: why should I remain a burden on you? Why should I always write with you holding my hand? My conscience and my pride rebel. I will be myself, faults and all."

In 1855, he wrote, "I have said in my heart, I wonder if Lucy Larcom will write to me, as she proposed? I should love to have her." Their correspondence continued until the time of his death.

[1] *Similitudes.*

CHAPTER IV.

REFLECTIONS OF A TEACHER.

It was not Miss Larcom's regular habit to keep a diary, but at certain times she recorded her thoughts in private note-books. Her object in doing this was to cultivate clearness of expression by frequently writing, and to give definiteness to her ideas by putting them down in black and white, thus preserving them, either for immediate use as material for letters to her friends, or for her own inspection years afterwards. Long intervals of time elapsed between the periods when she wrote in her diaries ; so they have not the value of a continuous life-history, but are interesting as records of phases of her thought which often reflect vividly the conditions in which she lived.

The following extracts from her diary have been made with the purpose of showing how she was influenced by the circumstances of her life, and how deeply she entered into the spirit of her intellectual and political surroundings.

Norton, May 4, 1860. Our talk has been of the mystics again to-day. With all the vagaries into which some of them wandered, I cannot help feeling that these men had more of the truth than any of those more strictly styled philosophers. Cousin has a cool, patronizing way with all systems that rather amuses me at times. What he says of the relation of philosophy to religion seems very conceited: that, while they have been separated, philosophy must now take religion by the hand, and gently guide her steps to the light. The history of philosophy would rather show that he was making a guide of the one who needed to be led! Certainly it must be so, if God is wiser than man.

May 21. Out of door studies, these past days, among goldfinches, orioles, larks, brown thrushes, and all the singing brotherhood; and a course of lectures on natural history, to help out the classifying and naming. Better living than among philosophers.

June 13. These weeks that have been spent over a discussion of Eastern and Western mythologies, have allowed little time for reading or thinking of anything else. I have learned to value the thoughts of thinkers, and to perceive the difference between them and pleasant surface-writers. I expected to gain much from Mrs. Child's "History of Religious Ideas," and I have found it full of entertaining and instructive facts, told in a very kind and impartial way; but hers is not the philosophic depth of Carlyle, nor the broad and deep spiritual insight of Maurice, — the latter always pours light into the windows of my soul, and makes truth seem all near and clear. Mrs. C.'s work is still a most valuable one, because it makes so much comprehensible that had been shut up for the general reader, and such a spirit as hers makes everything that she writes good to read. This reading and writing have impressed me more fully than ever before with the certainty that truth is one, radiating from one source through all manner of mediums, colored and distorted by all sorts of error; yet wherever a good word has been spoken, there is the voice of God, whether the speaker were Christian or Pagan.

June 20. After reading the addresses at the Music Hall, in memory of Theodore Parker, and what is said of him in the religious papers, it seems to me a great relief that there is a perfect Judge of human character and human life above. Neither friends nor foes could know this man truly; his works will follow him, right or wrong, for he wrote himself in innumerable hearts, with all the energy of confidence in his own views. I did not like the tone of his preaching and lecturing, — it seemed to me often dogmatic, and abusive of other beliefs; certainly never very patient with what he did not like. Yet the noble impulses he communicated, the perfect freedom of thought which he advised, cannot be without their good results. The fire will try his work, as it does and will that of all human workers, to prove of what sort it is.

August 12, Gardiner, Maine. Now in the seclusion of this little bird's nest in the woods, I feel easy and free, like the winds that sweep through pine and hemlock, and the birds that go singing or silent from the glen to the orchard. Heartsease grows here, best of all blossoms; I surely did not bring it with me, for I was very uneasy at home.

August 14. Leisure, — is it anything to be thankful for, or not? I never do what I mean to do, nor so much, as when I think my time all occupied. This vacation is almost gone, and not one of the achievements I had planned, in the way of writing, is executed. It is something to rest, but not so much, if one feels that it is not exactly right or necessary to rest!

August 18. The prospect of a journey to the mountains to-day. There is a thick fog from the river, but the birds are singing through it. I can scarcely let the summer go without giving me a glimpse of the mountains.

August 22. Returned last night after a very pleasant visit of three days. It rained on the way, but it was only the cooler and more comfortable traveling for that; and when the sun came out in the west just as we reached the top of a ridge from which the whole long mountain chain was visible on the horizon, I felt that that one view was enough compensation for going, and that first glimpse I shall never forget. The round summit of Blue, and the bolder ridges of Saddleback and Abraham, lifted themselves above the lower elevations that would be mountains anywhere but among mountains, far off and solemn with the deepening purple of sunset, and over them the sky hung, fiery gold, intermingled with shadow. The first glimpse was finer than anything afterward, though I rode up the lovely valley of the Sandy River, which is *like* a paradise, if not one, recalling ever the old words of the hymn: —

> "Sweet fields arrayed in living green,
> And rivers of delight."

What can be more beautiful than green meadow-lands, bordered by forest-covered slopes, that ever rise and rise, till they fade into dim blue mountain-distances?

I climbed one mountain half-way, — the bluest of the blue, — and so called, by emphasis, Mount Blue. It was a grand view, — the great distant mountain wall, and the valleys slumbering safe in its shadow. Yet the distant view is always more impressive, more full of suggestions for me; and coming back to the first point of observation, I hoped for a repetition of the first delight. But the far-off ridges were closely veiled with mist and rain, and a thunder-shower swept toward us from them, across the wide valley. Yet as we turned to leave, Mount Blue just lifted off his mist-cap for a few minutes, as if to say good-by!

Altogether, it is a most charming and comforting picture for future remembrance: flowery mountain-slopes, little garden patches of golden-rod, white everlasting and purple willow-herb, under the shade of maples, and firs, and graceful hemlocks; and glimpses of cottagers' homes on hillsides and by running streams. My eyes are rested, and my heart is glad.

August 24. Beverly. The sail down the Kennebec River was delightful, and I took a wicked sort of pleasure in shutting myself up from the crowd and enjoying it!

August 26. Sabbath day memories and regrets — how unlike everything else they are! One thing to be grateful for, in a Puritan training, is that it makes one day in the week a thoughtful one, at least. The old customs we may not keep up, — may even regard them as foolish, — still, there is a questioning as to right and wrong on this day, which we must be hardened to get wholly rid of. If I have lived unworthily for a week, the Sabbath quietly shows me myself in her mirror.

Lately I have heard some discussion as to the name and manner of keeping the day. "The Sabbath," they say, "was a Jewish institution, not a Christian festival, such as we should keep." But I believe that *rest* is still the noblest idea of the day; the old Sabbath was a type of Christian rest; not constrained, but free, full, peaceful; so I like not anything that disturbs the *quiet* of the day.

September 17. Whether such a record as this is a useful thing, or entirely useless, I begin to question. I don't want to feel interested in anything which is only to benefit myself, and I don't want to write these trifles for other people's eyes. A journal of the "subjective" kind I have always thought foolish, as nurturing a morbid self-consciousness in the writer; and yet, alone so much as I am, it is well to have some sort of a ventilator from the interior.

Letter-writing is a better safety valve than a journal, when we write to those we can trust, and this I meant to be a sort of prolonged letter, a mirror of my occupations and progress, for my old friend, Esther. But she, I fear, will never read it; she is on her way to a place of better occupation, and I feel that the first stimulus is gone.

Shall I stop in the middle of my book? No, I believe not; for I think it will be indirectly a useful thing, and I shall write just when I feel like it, often enough to keep track of myself, and give account of myself to myself.

Since I returned to school I have read — well, not much; two little works on natural history; I have begun Ruskin's fifth volume, with great interest, and Trench on the Parables for my Sunday class. "The Limits of Religious Thought" I am reading with a pupil, and with it Maurice's reply, "What is Revelation?" My impression of these two writers, so far, is that Maurice is a much more deeply religious man than Mansel; and that the latter's logic will not always sustain his footing. I do not like logic in religion, — reason is not always logic; reason seems to me to be the mind wide open — no faculty numb or asleep; and to that state of inner being, truth must come like sunshine, and the mysteries which cannot be explained will be harmonized with our certain knowledge, in such light.

September 22. Morris's Poems have come to me to-day, by mail. I have just glanced through the book, and find myself attracted by the clearness and simplicity of the songs; the most beautiful the most familiar, as songs should be. It does not strike me that any of them came from the very deep places of the heart, — many of them sound as if written only to please, and as if the highest aim of the author was to have them pretty and unobjectionable. I 've written things in that way myself sometimes, and I don't like it.

September 26. I know I have n't regarded ministers as others do, yet it seems to me that there are few "ministers" or "pastors" nowadays, — real ones, — such as the apostolic times knew. A "preacher" does not mean the thing, for he may preach himself only. I wonder whether the relations between pastor and people can ever be again as they have been? People are becoming their own judges and guides in religious things; this is a necessity of Protestantism, I think. And yet my "liberal" Mr. Maurice says that the "right of private judgment" only makes every man his own pope. The true idea of a church has not yet been shown the world, — a visible Church, I mean, — unless it was in the very earliest times; yes, the twelve disciples bound to their Lord in love, to do his work forever, — that was a church, — a Christian family. But then they had no system of theology to which all were expected to conform; love was all their theology. And then, afterwards, while they took the wisest and best as teachers, and called no one Master or Head but Christ, they were a true Church.

I don't believe we can look upon our ministers

as the early disciples did upon Paul and John, unless they have the spirit of Paul and John. The ministry is trifled with too much by ministers themselves, and it sometimes seems to me as if this was so, because it is made a *business*.

September 29. "Blessed are your eyes, for they see, and your ears, for they hear." This is the blessing of life: to be in the light and harmony of the love of God and reveal it. To "know the mysteries" of the kingdom of Heaven, — what is it, but to be in God's universe with a soul opened, by love, to truth; unto such only "it is given." Yet we have hearing and vision and the spiritual sense, all of us, and for the use of each, or misuse, or neglect, and consequent loss, every one is to blame. Oh, for a heart always opened; to read all parables in the light in which they were born!

November 10. I have actually forgotten to write for months in this book. I fear me, "my heart is nae here." I have lived a good deal in the past week, and the world has been doing a great business, — our country in particular. The Prince has turned the heads of our democratic people, and Republicans have chosen a President at last. That is glorious! Freedom takes long strides in these better days. The millennium is not so far off as we feared. While there is so much to be lived outside, who cares for the little self-life of a journal? But I never meant it to be a "subjective" one, and when it has been so, it has been so because I was living below my ideal. Yet this shall be just the book my thoughts shape from their various moods; when the thought is for myself, I will write it, and when it is for another, I will write it too.

"Whose window opened towards the rising sun."

So the happy pilgrim rested, knowing that as soon as there was light anywhere, he should have the first ray. Strange, that every Christian sojourner should not seek a room with windows opening to the dawn! Some of them seem afraid of the sun; they choose a chamber having only a black, northerly outlook, and lie down saying, "What a dreary, miserable world!" And what wonder that they should grow thin and sickly — plants of the shade must ever be so; the soul, as well as the body, needs large draughts of sunshine for vigorous life.

November 27. Since I came to Beverly I have been looking over "Wilhelm Meister" for the first time. I am disappointed in it, and have little respect for Goethe as a man, great as was his genius. Great thoughts he had, and they shine like constellations through the book; artistic, no doubt he was, but everything that relates to principle or right feeling is terribly chaotic, it seems to me. And *Wilhelm* is an embodiment of high-strung selfishness, under a cloak of generosity and spontaneous good feeling. If I could despise any man, it would be such a one as he.

December 9. God be thanked for the thinkers of good and noble thoughts! It wakes up all the best in ourselves, to come into close contact with others greater and better in every way than we are. Having just made myself the possessor of "Guesses at Truth," I feel as if I had struck a new mine, or were a privileged traveler into regions hitherto unknown, where there is every variety of natural and cultivated growth, where there are ever recurring contrasts of scenery, and where even the rocks are not barren, but glittering with veins of precious ore. How much better these "thinking books" are than any "sensation books" of any kind, prose or poetry! They are the true intellectual companions. One does not read them, and put them by on the shelf, to be read again one of these days, perhaps, — but they are wanted close at hand, and often.

"No spring nor summer beauty has such grace
As I have seen in an Autumnal face."

The poet Donne wrote so of the mother of "holy George Herbert." It is so true! and I have seen the same. It would be worth while to live long, to suffer much, to struggle and to endure, if one might have such spiritual beauty blossom out of furrows and wrinkles as has been made visible in aged human faces. Such countenances do not preach, — they are poetry, and music, and irresistible eloquence.

Christmas, 1860. Two or three books I have read lately. Mrs. Jameson's "Legends of the Madonna" is full of that fine appreciation of the deepest beauty, even in the imperfect creations of art, where the creation had in it the breath of spirit life, so peculiar to this gifted woman. If I were going to travel in Europe, I should want, next to a large historical knowledge, an intimate acquaintance with the writings of Mrs. Jameson, to appreciate the treasures of mediæval art.

Whittier's "Home Ballads," dear for friendship's sake, though not directly a gift from him, as were some of the former volumes. I wonder if that is what makes me like the songs in the "Panorama," — some of them — better than anything in this new volume, although I know that this is more perfect as poetry. I doubt if he will ever write anything that I shall like so well as the "Summer by the Lakeside," in that volume: it is so full of my first acquaintance with the mountains, and the ripening of my acquaintance with him, my poet-friend. How many blessings that friendship has brought me! — among them, a glimpse into a true home, a realizing of such brotherly and sisterly love as is seldom seen outside of books, — and best of all, the friendship of dear Lizzie, his sole home-flower, the meek lily blossom that cheers and beautifies his life. Heaven spare them long to each other, and their friendship to me!

But the "Ballads" are full of beauty and of a strong and steady trust, which grows more firmly into his character and poetry, as the years pass over him. "My Psalm," with its reality, its earnest depth of feeling, makes other like poems, Longfellow's "Psalm of Life," for instance, seem weak and affected. I like, too, the keenness and kindness of the Whitefield poem, in which he has preserved the memory of a Sabbath evening walk I took with him.

Dr. Croswell's poems contain many possibilities of poetry, and some realities; but there always seems to me a close air, as if the church windows were shut, in reading anything written by a devout Episcopalian. Still, there was true Christianity in the man, and it is also in the book.

December 27. To-night the telegraph reports the evacuation of Fort Moultrie by the Federal troops by order of the Executive, and the burning of the fort. There's something of the "spirit of '76" in the army, surely; South Carolina having declared herself a foe to the Union, how could those soldiers quietly give up one of the old strongholds to the enemy, even at the President's command?

But what will the end be? Is this secession-farce to end with a tragedy? The South will suffer, by insurrection and famine; there is every prospect of it; the way of transgressors is hard, and we must expect it to be so. God grant that, whatever must be the separate or mutual sufferings of North and South, these convulsions may prove to be the dying struggles of slavery, and the birth-throes of liberty.

It is just about a year since "Brown of Ossawatomie" was hung in the South, for unwise interference with slavery. He was not wholly a martyr; there were blood-stains on his hands, though no murder was in his heart. He was a brave man and a Christian, and his blood, unrighteously shed, still cries to heaven from the ground. Who knows but this is the beginning of the answer? But that judicial murder was not the only wrong for which the slaveholding South is now bringing herself before the bar of judgment, before earth and heaven. The secret things of darkness are coming to light, and the question will be decided rightly, I firmly believe. And the South is to be pitied, as all hardened and blinded wrong-doers should be! I believe the North will show herself a noble foe, if foe the South determines to make her.

CHAPTER V.

THE BEGINNING OF THE WAR.

January 20, 1861. I have run over the birth-histories of the nations of Europe, in their chaotic rise from barbarism; and have just completed a bird's-eye view of Italian mediæval history, with Koeppen's aid. The present history of Italy interests me greatly, and I would like to be able to link the present with the past. But what a debatable ground it has always been, and how unsparingly it has always been made mince-meat of, by all in authority there!

But all that history has revealed shows no more important epoch than the one in which we are living at this moment, in our unsettled and discordant Union. I hope it will come out plain and positive, as a question of right or wrong for every man to decide. It is so already, yet all will not see. So I hope that the demon of slavery, that "mystery of iniquity," will make his evil way evident, that we may return to no vile compact with sin.

February 28. The bluebirds have come! and the meadow-lark has sung over in the fields behind the garden, these two or three mornings. I have dreamed of spring these many nights, and now it is coming — coming!

What a blessing dreams are! I have heard birds sing, in bluer skies than May could show; doves have alighted on my head; violets, such as cannot be matched in any meadows for perfect tints and fragrance, have blossomed at my feet; have wept for joy at the sublime beauty of Alps grander than any real Alps, — which I would yet fain see, though I shall not, with these eyes, — all this in my winter dreams. Through dreams, we must always believe in a deeper and more perfect beauty than we know. The world is lovely, but there is a lovelier, else we could not see what we do in sleep. The glory of living is that life *is* glorious beyond all our possible imaginations, — the eternal life, — the "glory that shall be revealed" in us.

March 2. What does cause depression of spirits? Heavy head and heavy heart, and no sufficient reason for either, that I know of. I am out of doors every day, and have nothing unusual to trouble me; yet every interval of thought is clouded; there is no rebound, no rejoicing as it is my nature to rejoice, and as all things teach me to do. We are strange phenomena to ourselves, when we will stop to gaze at ourselves; but that I do not believe in; there are pleasanter subjects, and self is a mere speck on the great horizon of life.

A new volume of poems by T. B. Aldrich, just read, impresses me especially with its daintiness and studied beauty. There are true flashes of poetry, but most carefully trimmed and subdued, so as to shine artistically. I believe the best poetry of our times is growing too artistic; the study is too visible. If freedom and naturalness are lost out of poetry, everything worth having is lost.

March 3. Eternal life and eternal death; what do these words mean? This is the question that comes up again and again. It has recently been brought up by those whom I am appointed to instruct; and the question with its answer, brings new and fearful responsibility with every return. I am more and more convinced that the idea of *duration* is not the one that affects us most: for here it has proved that those who are least careful about what they are in heart and life, are trying hardest to convince themselves and others that the "doctrine of eternal punishment" is not true. By making themselves believe that to be the all-important question, they draw off their own and others' attention from the really momentous one, — "Am I living the eternal life? Is it begun in me now?"

And now I see why I have questioned whether it was right in me to express my own doubts of this very doctrine. The final renovation of all souls, their restoration to life in holiness and love, is certainly a hope of mine that is not without a strong infusion of confidence; but I dare not say it is a belief; because both reason and revelation have left it in deep mystery; and the expression of any such belief does not seem to me likely to help others much; certainly not those who are indolent or indifferent regarding the true Christian life.

Then the "loss of the soul" is in plain language spoken of by our Lord as possible. What can that mean, but the loss of life in Him? the loss of ennobling aspirations, of the love of all good, of the power of seeing and seeking truth? And if this is possible to us now, by our own choice, why not forever? — since, as free beings, our choice must always be in our own power?

The truth that we must all keep before us, in order to be growing better forever, is that life is love and holiness; death, selfishness and sin; then it is a question of life and death to be grappled with in the deep places of every soul.

March 5. I cannot let this birthday pass without a memorial of its sun's rising and setting on flower-gifts from these my girl-friends: a wreath hung on my door in the morning, and a bouquet left in my room at night. It brings spring to my spirit earlier than I expected; pleasant it is to receive any token of love; and gifts like these come so seldom, that when they do come, I am sure they mean love. And with them comes the assurance of a deeper summer-warmth, — the arousing of all high and holy feelings in the deep places of the soul yet winter-sealed. "My shriveled heart" shall yet "recover greenness." I could not feel this "deadly cold" that sometimes pierces me, if incapable of warmth. It may not be in an earthly clime that my nature shall blossom out freely and fully into heavenly light; but the time will come.

Yesterday was the inauguration: we have a

President, a country: and we are "the Union" still, and shall so remain, our President thinks. But I doubt whether the pride of slavery will ever bow to simple freedom, as it must, if the self-constituted aliens return. There is a strange new chapter in the world's history unfolding to-day; we have not half read it yet.

Sabbath, April 14, 1861. This day broke upon our country in gloom; for the sounds of war came up to us from the South, — war between brethren; civil war; well may "all faces gather blackness." And yet the gloom we feel ought to be the result of sorrow for the erring, for the violators of national unity, for those who are in black rebellion against truth, freedom, and peace. The rebels have struck the first blow, and what ruin they are pulling down on their heads may be guessed, though not yet fully foretold; but it is plain to see that a dark prospect is before them, since they have no high principle at the heart of their cause.

It will be no pleasure to any American to remember that he lived in this revolution, when brother lifted his hand against brother; and the fear is, that we shall forget that we are brethren still, though some are so unreasonable and wander so far from the true principles of national prosperity. Though the clouds of this morning have cleared away into brightness, it seems as if we could feel the thunder of those deadly echoes passing to and from Fort Sumter. But there is a right, and God always defends it. War is not according to His wish; though it seems one of the permitted evils yet. He will scatter those who delight in it, and it is not too much to hope and expect that He will uphold the government which has so long been trying to avert bloodshed.

Another unpleasant association with this day. I went to the meeting expecting and needing spiritual food, and received only burning coals and ashes. There was a sermon (not by our minister, I am glad to say) to prove that Satan will be tormented forever and ever; and the stress of the argument was to prove the *endlessness* of his punishment. The text was taken from the twentieth of Revelation, a chapter which few have the audacity to explain; but the object was to show that "eternal," in its highest sense, is not so plainly taught in the Bible, as "eternal" in its lowest sense, that of duration. Truly, "The wisdom of men is foolishness with God!" — the deep and sacred truth of eternal life lies hidden yet in the words of Christ, for him who will understand. It seems to me wrong to preach a theoretical sermon like this to those who are hungering for the bread of life; who are longing to come nearer to the Saviour, and receive His spirit. I think none but a young minister would have preached so; certainly, a warm-hearted Christian could not have treated the subject in that cold argumentative way. As it was, I could only pity one who could so misinterpret his Master's words; he must be yet on the outer threshold of the heart of Christ, if so near as that, and not, like the Beloved John, leaning on His bosom. And I grieved for the "hungry sheep," who looked up and were not fed. But if such sermons drive all hearers to the word itself, refusing human interpretations, they may do good. Alas! We grope in darkness yet! Man is blinded to God's deep meaning everywhere, in thought and in life, in religion and in government. The dark ages are not wholly past; nor will they be, until all fetters of thought and limb are broken.

Yet, through all, the birds are singing with the joy of sunshine after April rain; and earth is beautiful and bright, beneath the promises of spring,— written on soft skies and sweet west winds. The good God sits yet upon His throne of love!

April 21. The conflict is deepening; but thanks to God, there is no wavering, no division, now, at the North! All are united, as one man; and from a peaceful, unwarlike people, we are transformed into an army, ready for the battle at a moment's warning.

The few days I have passed in Boston this week are the only days in which I ever carried my heart into a crowd, or hung around a company of soldiers with anything like pleasure. But I felt a soldier-spirit rising within me, when I saw the men of my native town armed and going to risk their lives for their country's sake; and the dear old flag of our Union is a thousand times more dear than ever before. The streets of Boston were almost canopied with the stars and stripes, and the merchants festooned their shops with the richest goods of the national colors.

And now there are rumors of mobs attacking our troops, of bridges burnt, and arsenals exploded, and many lives lost. The floodgates of war are opened, and when the tide of blood will cease none can tell.

May 6. Through the dark and lurid atmosphere of war the light of "Nature's own exceeding peace" still softly falls on the earth. The violets have opened their blue eyes by the roadside; the saxifrage fringes the ledges with white; and the arbutus, the Pilgrim's mayflower, blossoms on the hills away from here; we have no hillsides for it to grow upon, but I had some on May-day, from the hills of Taunton. How strange the contrast between these delicate blossoms and the flaring red flower of war that has burst into bloom with the opening of spring!

Every day brings something to stir the deep places of the soul, and in the general awakening of life and liberty it may be that every heart feels its own peculiar sorrow and happiness more keenly. There is a deeper life in every breath I draw; and messages from distant friends seem more near and touching. One day, from one of the most beloved and honored, comes a kind word for my poor efforts at poetry; almost a prophecy of some blessed days of summer life among the mountains by and by, —and a holy benediction, "God bless thee, and keep thee!" that fell upon my heart like the first ray of some new and unknown morning. All life seemed green and glowing with a freshened trust. God is, and goodness is; and true hearts are, forever! There is nothing to doubt, even in these dark days!

Then, the next day, a message from dear Esther (she could not write it herself) to say that she is dying, and wants to hear from me again. And to think that she had been drooping all these spring days, while I have been too full of occupation with the stir of the times to write! But she says my words have always been good for her, and surely few have blessed me by life and thought as she has. Heaven will have one bond for my heart, closer than any yet. I am glad that she can lie down in peace, before the horrible scenes of bloodshed, which only a miracle can now avert, shall be enacted.

May 9. I had set myself to reading Maury's "Physical Geography of the Sea," after a long deferring; but now that he has come out as a rank rebel against his country, I cannot feel any interest in his theories, ingenious as they are said to be. Like poor, wise, fallen Bacon, his ideas may prove something to the world, "after some years have passed over," but one is not fond of being taught by traitors.

May 15. A glimpse into a heart which has always been closed, both to God and man, — what a chaos it discloses! Yet with all the elements of order there, it is like the promise of a new creation.

Such a glimpse, such a half-unveiling, one has given me to-day, out of a soul-deep, long-repressed longing for "something to love!" Ah, that sorrowful need of every woman's heart, especially; yet more joyful than sorrowful, because the longing shows the fulfillment possible, — yes, certain. In the heavenly life, which such aspirations prophesy, there is love abounding, to give and to receive. And I am thankful for one more to love.

May 20. Esther dead! Gone home two days before I heard or dreamed of it! But since she has gone home,— since it is only a glorious release for her, — I will not let a thought of repining sully the gladness I ought to share with her. It is only that one who has always lived near the Holiest One is now called nearer still. I have known her only in Him, and there I know her and love her still.

May 22. They write to me of her funeral, of the white flowers beside her head, and of her own lilies of the valley strewn over her in the grave by one who knew how she loved them. Everything that would have made her happy, had her eyes been open to see, and her ears to hear. They sang the hymns she loved, "Rock of Ages," and "I would not live alway," and "Thy will be done." And my dear friend is free! — her soul has blossomed into heavenly light! I told her once that this book was for only her to see; I do not like my thoughts when I think them for myself alone; and there is no other friend who would care as she cared. Will she read them now?

May 27. This is the gala week of spring. None of the early flowers have quite faded, and the apple-trees are in full bloom, while elms and maples are just wearing their lightest drapery of green, so tardily put on. Soft breezes, sweet melody from many birds, clear sunshine, not yet too warm, — all things are just in that state, when, if we could wish for a standstill in nature, we should.

And Esther has been one week in heaven! It seems to me, sometimes, as if some new charm was added to cloud and sunshine, and spring blossoms, since she went away; as if it were given me to see all things clearer for her clearer vision; she would speak to me, if she could.

Lectures these few days on historical women. Paula, Queen Elizabeth, and Madame de Maintenon, thus far. Paula, the friend of St. Jerome, and the woman whom the speaker made to illustrate friendship, pleased me most, as presenting a higher ideal than either of the others. Christianity gave woman the privilege of a pure friendship with man; before unknown, we are told. It is one of the noblest gifts of religion, and I wish people believed in it more thoroughly. But only a truly elevated and chastened nature can understand real friendship, — not a Platonic ideal only, though that is elevated, let who will sneer at it: but a drawing of the noblest souls together, and to the Soul of souls, for the highest ends. This is Christian friendship; union in Christ for all beauty, all purity, all true and noble life, which He illustrated in His own glorious life and death, and of which He is now the inspiring power. "We are complete in Him."

Yes, I am sure that it is in drawing near to Him that I feel the loveliness of such beauty as that into which the world now blossoms; for is not He the Lord of nature, and also my Lord and Friend? And through His great love for us, I see the ideal of all true human love. "As I have loved you," He said, "so must we love each other, with tenderness, forbearance, generosity, and self-sacrifice."

Such friendship is possible, is eternal; and it is almost the most precious thing in the soul's inheritance.

June 12. I have been free for a few days, and have taken a journey, — a flying tour among some of my friends. How it quieted me, to be with my peace-loving friends in these wild times of war!

There are some friends whose presence is encouragement in all that is good, whom to look upon is to grow stronger for the truth. There are homes, too, over which saintly memories hang, making all within and around them sacred, blending earth with heaven by holy sympathies. How blessed I am, to know such friends, to enter such homes as these! Sometimes I can truly say, "My cup runneth over!"

June 14. Still the same old weariness of study; "weariness of the flesh." Books are treasures, but one may work among treasures even, digging and delving, till there is little enjoyment in them. And the greater pain is, that, by becoming numb to the beautiful and true, in any form, one does not feel its power entirely, anywhere. So I felt this morning, which I stole from my books. I sat on a ledge in a distant field, all around me beautiful with June, and no sight or sound of human care in sight. I sat there like a prisoner, whose chains had dropped for the moment, but the weight and pain of them lingered still. Yet I began to feel what it is to be free, and how sweet and soothing nature always is, before I rose to return. I think it would not take me long to get accustomed to freedom, and to rejoice in it with exceeding joy.

June 23. Weary, weary, too weary to listen patiently to the heavy Sabbath bells; far too weary to sit in the church and listen to loud words and loud singing. And my brain is too tired to let my heart feel the beauty of this quiet day. I only know that the balm and beauty of June are around me, without realizing it much. But rest will come soon, up among the mountains with friends who love noise and confusion as little as I do. I shall be at peace. A blessing will come to us, among the hills.

July 4. Crackers all around the house at night. Fire-crackers, torpedoes, pistols, and bell-ringing, are enough to make one sick of one's country, if this is the only way of showing one's patriotism. I am sure, as I lay last night, nervously wide awake, with every shot startling and paining me as if it had really gone through my brain, I felt more belligerently disposed toward the young patriots than toward the Southern rebels! But if there is no other way of nursing an interest in free institutions among these juvenile republicans, there's nothing to be done but to endure the "Fourth of July" once a year, for the general good.

August 1. Yesterday I visited the residence of the late Hon. Daniel Webster, at Marshfield. There was much that was interesting to see in the great man's home; I think the two things that pleased me most were the portraits of his mother, and his black cook, or housekeeper. The latter was a fine painting, the face so full of intelligence, gratitude, and all good feelings; and there was an evidence of the true sympathy and home comfort between master and servant, if it is well to use those words, in the picture itself, the care with which it was painted, as well as the speaking face. The other was simply an old-fashioned cut profile, in black outline, and underneath it the words, "My excellent mother — D. Webster."

Out of doors, the wonderful old elm was the greatest attraction, with its branches sweeping the ground, and making an arbor and a cathedral at once, before the threshold. Webster himself — but it is not well to call up anything but pleasant memories of the dead; and these do linger about the home he loved. What the nation thinks of him may be recorded elsewhere.

August 2. I visited Plymouth, placed my foot

on the memorable "Plymouth Rock," of the Pilgrims (now so enclosed and covered as to leave scarcely space sufficient for my large foot to rest upon), looked at Mayflower curiosities in the hall, books, shoes, and fans of the olden time, and more especially pewter platters, which, judging from some ancient will I looked over in the Court House, were the most important personal property of the Puritans. John Alden's well-worn Bible was open at the date of publication, 1620, so he had it new for his westward voyage; I wondered whether it was the gift of some friend left behind, or his own purchase. Miles Standish's long rapier was scarcely more interesting to me than the big kettle labeled with his name, which might have supplied the colony with dinner, judging from its size. Some old documents relating to the Quakers caught my attention; one especially, wherein Winthrop demurred from signing his name to a report of Commissioners, wherein this troublesome sect were adjudged worthy to be put to death for their "cursed opinions and devilish tennets," — Winthrop signed, leaving testimony beside his name, that it was "as a querry, not as an act." Coming back to George Fox's journal, which I had borrowed for vacation reading, I could not but smile at the difference a hundred or two years will make; I can admire both Puritan and Quaker for their sincerity, and only wish they could have understood each other better. There is no defense for the persecution of the "Fathers," except the imperfection of human nature, and there is only this for the misguided ways into which the Quakers were led, by mistaking their own fancies for the "inner light." Better death on both sides (for what each held to be truth) than indifference to truth. And, stepping among the bones of the Pilgrims, on Burying Hill, and looking away over the waves which brought them and freedom to New England, and so to the Union, I could not but contrast the struggle of that day with the present war for liberty against oppression. It is, in reality, the "Old Colony" against the "Old Dominion," or rather, the latter against the former, aristocracy against the republic. God will prosper us now as then; but perhaps we are to be brought as low before Him as they were, before our cause can be victorious.

August 3. Fishing on the "Indian Pond" in Pembroke half the day, catching sunfish and shiners, red perch and white; my first exploits of the kind. It is a pleasant day to remember, for the green trees and the blue waters, for lilies wide awake on the bosom of the waters in the morning sunshine, for fresh breezes, and for pleasant company.

August 11. At Amesbury, — with two of the dearest friends my life is blessed with, — dear quiet-loving Lizzie, and her poet brother. I love to sit with them in the still Quaker worship, and they love the free air and all the beautiful things as much as they do all the good and spiritual.

The harebells nodding in shade and shine on the steep banks of the Merrimac, the sparkle of the waters, the blue of the sky, the balm of the air, and the atmosphere of grave sweet friendliness which I breathed for one calm "First-day" are never to be forgotten.

August 20. One of the stillest moonlight evenings, — not a sound heard but the bleat of a lamb, and the murmur of the river; all the rest a cool, broad, friendly mountainous silence. Peace comes down with the soft clouds and mists that veil the hills; the Pemigewasset sings all night in the moonshine, and I lie and dream of the beauty of those hill-outlines around Winnipiseogee, that I looked upon with so satisfied a greeting from the car window on my way hither. The mountains do not know their own beauty anywhere but by a lakeside. So it is: beauty sets us longing for other beauty; the clouds moving above their summits suggest possibilities that earthly summits, at their grandest, can never attain. And no dream can suggest the possibilities of the beautiful that "shall be revealed."

August 24. "The eye is not satisfied with seeing, and the ear with hearing," and one can never tire of the vision of mountain landscapes, and the quiet song of summer rivers. Every day since I have been here in this beautiful village of Campton, I have driven through some new region; sometimes into the very heart of the hills, where nothing is to be seen but swelling slopes on every side, hills which have not quite attained mountainhood, but which would be mountains anywhere but in the "Granite State;" and sometimes out into the interval openings of the river; with new views of "Alps on Alps" on the northern horizon, the gate of the Franconia Notch opening dimly afar with its mountain haystacks piled beside it. It is rest to soul and body to be among these mountains; one thing only is lacking; the friends I had hoped to see here are not with me. But too much joy is not to be looked for; let me hope that they are among scenes more beautiful, and with dearer friends than I. Yet how delightful it would have been, to be with the best friends, among the most beautiful scenes.

August 25. I am enjoying the society of my old friend and former associate teacher. She is more gifted than I, in most ways, and it is pleasant to talk to some one who, you take it for granted, has a clearer understanding, and deeper insight, and more adequate expression than yourself.

August 28. Yesterday a rare treat; a ride to Waterville (to the "end of the wood" as they speak of it here) in a three-seated open wagon. I wish they would have only open ones for mountain travel.

September 5. Why do I not love to be near the sea better than among the mountains? Here is my home, if birthplace makes home. But no, it is not my natural preference; I believe I was born longing after the mountains. And rivers and lakes are better to me than the ocean. I remember how beautiful the Merrimac looked to me in childhood, the first true river I ever knew; it opened upon my sight and wound its way through my heart like a dream realized; its harebells, its rocks, and its rapids, are far more fixed in my memory than anything about the sea. Yet the vastness and depth and the changes of mist and sunshine are gloriously beautiful; I know and feel their beauty. Still, I admire it most in glimpses; a bit of blue between the hills, only a little more substantial than the sky, and a white sail flitting across it; or when it is high-tide calm, — one broad, boundless stillness, — then there is rest in the sea, but it never rests me like the strong silent hills; they bear me up on their summits into heaven's own blue eternity of peace. But is it right to wrap one's own being in this mantle of peace, while the country is ravaged by war? — its garments rolled in blood, brother fighting against brother to the death? The tide of rebellion surges higher and higher, and there is no sadder proof that we are not the liberty-loving people that we used to call ourselves, than to learn that there are traitors in the secret councils of the nation, in forts defended by our own bravest men; among women, too: "Sisters! oh, Sisters! Shame o' ladies!" A disloyal woman at the North, with everything woman ought to hold dear at stake in the possible fall of this government, — it is too shameful! I hope every one such will be held in "durance vile" until the war is over.

But will it end until the question is brought to its true issue, — liberty or slavery? I doubt it: and I would rather the war should last fifty years, than ever again make the least compromise with slavery, that arch-enemy of all true prosperity, that eating sin of our nation. Rather divide at once, rather split into a thousand pieces, than sink back into this sin!

The latest news is of the capture of the Hatteras Forts, a great gain for us, and a blight to privateering at the South; — with a rumor of "Jeff Davis's" death, which nobody believes because it is so much wished. Yet to his friends he is a man, and no rebel. War is a bitter curse, — it forbids sympathy, and makes us look upon our enemies as scarcely human; and we cannot help it, when our foes are the foes of right.

Norton, September 8. Am I glad for trials, for disappointments, for opportunities for self-sacrifice, for everything God sends? Ah! indeed I do not know! How many times, when we say, "Try me, and know my heart," the answer is, 'Ye know not what ye ask!" And I know not why, in some states of mind and body, what *seems* a very little trouble (or would, if told another), should be so oppressive.

But "little," and "great," in the world's vocabulary, are very different terms from what they are in individual experience; and submission, and grateful acquiescing obedience to divine will, are to be learned by each in his own capacity. Two weeks ago, I was saying over to myself, every day, as if it were a new thought, Keble's lines, —

> "New treasures still, of countless price,
> God will provide for sacrifice."

And as those words kept recurring, as if whispered by a spirit, I thought I should be glad to have my best treasures to give for sacrifice, to make others happy with what was most precious to me. And as my way seemed uncertain, and for a day or two I knew not whether to move or to sit still, I said, "Lead me! Behold the handmaid of the Lord; let it be unto me according to Thy will, — only let me do nothing selfishly." And the answer came in the withdrawal of a blessing from me; no doubt with purposes of greater blessing to some one, somewhere and somehow; and I am only half reconciled as yet. Shall I ever believe that God knows best, and does what is best for me, and for us all? It is easy enough in theory, but these great and little trials tell us the truth about ourselves, — show us our insincerity. And now I close this record, which has been my nearest companion for so many months. Esther is gone. Is there any friend who cares enough for me just as I am, to keep it in memory of me? Or had I better bury it from my own eyes and all others'? It may be good for me to read the record of myself as I have been, — cheerful or morbid, — and of what I have read, thought, and done, wisely or unwisely. The "Country Parson" thinks a diary a good thing; and I do too, in many ways, but I would rather write for a friend's kindly eyes than for my own: even about myself. Therefore letters are to me a more genial utterance than a journal, and I would write any journal as if for some one who could understand me fully, love me, and have patience with me through all. I do not know if now there is any such friend for me; yet dear friends I have, and more and more precious to me, every year. If these were my last words, I would set them down as a testimony to the preciousness of human friendships; dearer and richer than anything else on earth. By them is the revelation of the divine in the human; by them heaven is opened, truth is made clear, and life is worth the living. So have I been blessed, drawn heavenward by saintly messengers in the garb of mortality. So shall it be forever, for true love is — eternal, it is life itself.

September 12. Is it always selfish to yield to depression? Can one help it, if the perspective of a coming year of lonely labor seems very long? No. I shall not be alone; I shall feel the sympathy of all the good and true, though apart from them; and though I cannot come very near to any under this roof, yet to all I can come nearer than I think I can. And by and by these strange restless yearnings will be stilled; I shall quiet my soul in the peace of God. He has said, "I will never leave thee nor forsake thee!" Oh! what is any woman's life worth without the friendship of the One ever near, the only divine?

Yes, I will make my work my friend. My trials,

my vexations, my cares, shall speak good words to me, and I will not blind my eyes to the beauty close at hand, because of the lost glory of my dreams. I wish I could be more to all these young glad beings, — it is not in me to touch the chords of many souls at once, but I will enlarge my sympathies.

October 5, 1861. This first week of October, this month of months, shall not pass without some record of its beauty. Norton woods and Norton sunsets are the two redeeming features of the place; as its levelness is its bane. What is it in us that refuses to love levels? Is it that there is no searching and toiling for anything, up cool heights and down in sheltered hollows?

These splendidly tinted maples before my window would be a hundred-fold more splendid if lifted up among the hemlocks and pines of the mountain-sides. Oh! how magnificent those New Hampshire hills must be now, in the sunset of the year!

The place is a level, and boarding-school life is a most wearisome level to me, yet flowers spring up, and fruits grow in both. We are to welcome "all that makes and keeps us low;" yet it seems to me as if it would be good for me to ascend oftener to the heights of being; I fear losing the power and the wish to climb.

Let us say we are struggling to put down slavery, and we shall be strong.

October 8. Yesterday two letters came to me, each from a friend I have never seen, yet each with a flower-like glow and perfume that made my heart glad. And at evening a graceful little basket of fruit was left in my room, and this morning a bunch of fringed gentians, blue with the thoughtfulness of the sky that hangs over the far solitary meadows, the last answer from earth to heaven from the frosty fields.

October 11. Rain: and just one of those dreary drizzling rains which turn one in from the outer world upon one's own consciousness, — a most unhealthy pasture land for thought, in certain states of mind and body. Just how far we should live in self-consciousness, and how far live an outside life, or rather, live in the life of others, is a puzzle. Without something of an inner experience, it is not easy to enter into other lives, to their advantage; some self-knowledge is necessary, to keep us from intruding upon others; but it is never good to make self the centre of thought.

October 13. George Fox's journal is a leaf from a strange chapter of the world's history: from the history of religion. If a plain man should come among us now, asking leave of none to speak, but "testifying" in religious assemblies to the reality of the inward life of light and peace in Christ, his blunt and simple ways might be unpleasing to many, but every scoffer would look on, more with wonder than with anger. Many, I am sure, would welcome such a voice of sincerity and "livingness," sounding through the outward services of religion. The days of religious persecution can scarcely return again; nor, it is to be hoped, the days of those strange phenomena which so irritated our ancestors; men walking as "signs" to the people, declaring their dreams to be visions from God, and uttering wild, unmeaning prophecies for inspiration. How hard it is to learn what "true religion and undefiled" is! *Life* is a better word for this universal bond than *religion*. And we shall see, sometime, that it is only by the redemption of all our powers, all that is in us and in the outward world, that we are truly "saved." We must receive the true light through and through, we must keep our common sense, our talents, our genius, just the same; — only that light must glow through all, to make all alive. And when home, and friendships, and amusements, and all useful and beautiful thoughts and things are really made transparent with that divine light, when nothing that God has given us is rejected as "common or unclean," the "new heaven and the new earth" will have been created, and we shall live in our Creator and Redeemer.

The great difference between the early Quakers and the Puritans seems to me to be that the former had larger ideas of truth, deeper and broader revelations, yet mixed with greater eccentricities, as might be expected. The Puritans were most anxious for a place where they could worship undisturbed, as their consciences dictated; the Quakers were most desirous that the Word of Life should be spoken everywhere, — the Light be revealed to all. Each made serious mistakes,—what else could we expect, from the best that is human? And the errors of both were, in great part, the errors of the age,—intolerance and fanaticism.

October 12. How refreshing the clear cold air is, after the summer-like fogs and rains we have had! I love the cold; the northern air is strengthening; it has the breath of the hills in it, the glow of Auroral lights, and the purity of the eternal snows. There is little of the south in my nature; the north is my home; Italy and the tropics will do for dream excursions; I should long for the sweeping winds of the hillsides, if I were there.

October 15. The beauty of this morning was wonderful; something in the air made me feel like singing. I thought my weariness was all gone; but leaning over books brought it back. After school four of us rode off in the wagon through the woods; and delighted ourselves with the sunset, the katydids, and the moonlight.

October 22. I heard Charles Sumner on the Rebellion: my first sight and hearing of the great anti-slavery statesman. He was greeted with tremendous applause, and every expression of opposition to slavery was met with new cheers. He does not seem to me like a man made to awaken enthusiasm; a great part of his address was statistical, and something we all knew before,—the long preparation of this uprising of the rebels; and his manner was not that of a man surcharged with his subject, but of one who had thoroughly and elegantly prepared himself to address the people. At this time we are all expecting orators to speak as we feel, — intensely; perhaps it is as well that all do not meet our expectations. One idea which he presented seemed to me to be worth all the rest, and worth all the frothy spoutings for "Union" that we hear every day; it was that our battalions must be strengthened by *ideas*, by *the* idea of freedom. That is it. Our men do not know what they are fighting for; freedom is greater than the Union, and a Union, old or new, with slavery, no true patriot will now ask for. May we be saved from that, whatever calamities we may endure!

The ride to and from Boston has a new picture since summer: the camp at Readville, just under the shadow of the Milton hills. It is a striking picture, the long array of white tents, the soldiers marching and countermarching, and the hills, tinted with sunset and autumn at once, looking down upon the camping ground. Little enough can one realize what war is, who sees it only in its picturesque aspect, who knows of it only by the newspapers, by knitting socks for soldiers, and sewing bed-quilts for the hospitals. I should give myself in some more adequate way, if we were definitely struggling for freedom; for there is more for women to do than to be lookers-on.

October 27. Looking out on the clouds at sunset, the thought of God as constantly evolving beauty from His own being into all created forms, struck me forcibly, as the right idea of our lives; that, like Him, we should be full of all truth and love, and so grow into beauty ourselves, and impart loveliness to all we breathe upon, or touch. Inspiration from Him is all we have to impart in blessing to others.

What is the meaning of these moods and states that fetter some of us so? I have seen life just as I see it now, and been glad in it, while for many months all things have brought me a nightmare-feeling that I could not shake off. I know it is the same world, the same life, the same God; I do not doubt Him, nor the great and good ends that He is working out for all; yet nothing wears its old delight.

October 30. "And with a child's delight in simple things." That I have not lost all this, I felt to-day, in receiving a note from an unknown person, — from one who had read some poems of mine in childhood, and now, a woman, bears something not unworthy the name of poet; to hear some new voice speaking to me in this way, as a friend, is pleasant to me. I have written as I have felt, in my verses; they have been true words from my deepest life, often; and I am glad whenever they call forth a sincere answer, as now; — one word of real appreciation repays me for pages of mere fault-finding. Yet a kind fault-finder is the best of friends.

What is the meaning of "gossip?" Does n't it originate with sympathy, an interest in one's neighbor, degenerating into idle curiosity and love of tattling? Which is worse, this habit, or keeping one's self so absorbed intellectually as to forget the sufferings and cares of others, to lose sympathy through having too much to think about?

October 31. I must hurry my mind, when I have to press ancient history into a three-months' course, and keep in advance of my class in study, with rhetoric and mental philosophy requiring a due share of attention besides, and the whole school to be criticised in composition and furnished with themes.

November 5. Governor Andrew's proclamation was a very touching one. Thanksgiving will be a sad day this year, yet a more sacred day than ever. I read his allusion to the Potomac, as now a sacred river to us, since the blood of our soldiers had mingled with its waters; and we felt that one throb of patriotism unites us all, however we must suffer.

November 7. Frémont is removed! It seems too bad, for none could awaken enthusiasm as he did, everywhere. And yet military law is all that holds us up now, and we have to trust blindly that the rulers are right. It may prove to be so, but to withdraw him when within a few miles of the enemy seems too hard. We shall respect him all the more, to see him bearing it nobly for his country's sake.

November 14. The best news for us since the war began has come within a day or two; and it is confirmed. Beaufort, S. C., is taken by a federal fleet, and the secessionists are in real consternation. All agree that this is a decisive blow, and if we can maintain our position, the war will end speedily. But after that, there will be the same question to settle — "Are we one country or not?" We shall not be any more agreed than we were before, until slavery is abolished. The idea that the negroes are attached to the "institution" is well shown up now, when two hundred slaves, the property of one man in the very heart of slavedom, hasten at once to board our war steamers for protection; and when their masters vainly try to whip them before them in their retreat. If now our government undertakes to cultivate cotton by free labor of colored men, it will be a grand step towards the general liberation. And if thus the South can be made to honor labor, we may by and by be reunited in spirit; for that is the element of separation. We are carried onward in a way we little know, and it is impossible not to rejoice when we feel ourselves borne by a mighty and loving Power towards a glorious goal.

November 18. Much of our Christianity is not of a sufficiently enlarged type to satisfy an educated Hindoo; not that Unitarianism is necessary, for that system has but a surface-liberalism which can become very hard, and finally very narrow, as its history among us has often proved. It is not a system at all that we want: it is Christ, the "wisdom of God and the power of God," Christ, the loving, creating, and redeeming friend of the world, Christ, whose large, free being enfolds all that is beautiful in nature and in social life; and all that is strong and deep and noble in the sanctuary of every living soul. When Christians have truly learned Christ, they can be true teachers.

November 24. Thanksgiving is over; I have been to Beverly and returned. I am glad they wanted me so much, for I should not have gone without; and in this place there is little in harmony with our best home festival. Our governor's proclamation was of the true Puritan stamp; and the day was one to be kept religiously, in view of our present national troubles, and of the strong Power that is bearing us through and over them. We are sure that God is on our side; and one of the things to be most thankful for is that the desire for the liberation of the slave is becoming universal. Our armies, that began to fight for Union alone, now see that Union is nothing without freedom, and when this Northern heart is fully inspired with that sentiment the Northern hand will strike a decisive blow; such a blow as only the might of right can direct.

November 25. The first snow! Light and thick as swan's-down, it wraps the shivering bosom of mother earth. Last night I went to sleep with an uncurtained window before me, and the still, bright stars looking in; I awoke to find the air dim and heavy with snow, and all the treetops bending in graceful gratitude; and to think aloud the lines, —

> "Oh! if our souls were but half as white
> As the beautiful snow that fell last night!"

I do not like this vague kind of unrest, and this dissatisfaction with myself which returns so often. I am willing to be dissatisfied, but I want to know exactly with what, that I may mend. I believe the trouble partly is that I do not, cannot, love very much the people that I see oftenest. Their thoughts and ways are so different from mine I cannot comfortably walk with them. It seems to me as if we were like travelers on the same journey, but in paths wide apart; and we can only make one another hear by effort and shouting. Whether this is wrong, or simply one of the things that cannot be helped, I cannot clearly see; but I am afraid that I am too willing to excuse myself for so doing.

November 26. The last day of school; my classes all examined, and to-morrow we scatter, to gather ourselves together again in two weeks. I am not sure whether I like or dislike these frequent changes; on the whole I think I like them; for they break up the monotony, and then one does get so totally glued to the manner of school life: there is no better name for the cohesive power that makes us one household for the time. I do not believe it possible (for me, at least, and I doubt whether it is for any woman) to have quite a home feeling, among the many living together, in a place like this. There is not expansive power enough in me to take in all.

Beverly, December. The two weeks of vacation are nearly over, and I have done nothing but sew. I had planned to read, and paint, and walk, and rest; but things are as they are, and one cannot go in tatters. I like to be somewhat troubled and absorbed in the necessities of life, *once in a while;* it is rather pleasant than otherwise to feel that something urgently requires my attention; and then this is the way to realize how three fourths of the inhabitants of this world live to eat, drink, and wear clothes.

December 13. Vacation is over; and here I am at Norton again, not so fully awake and in earnest about school work as I wish I was.

My whole life has lost the feeling of reality; I cannot tell why. Alike in the city, by the sea-shore, and here on the levels of this now leafless flat-land, I feel as if I were "moving about in worlds unrealized." I know well enough the theory of life; what principles must sustain me; what great objects there are to live for; and still there remains the same emptiness, the same wonder in everything I do. I feel as I imagine the world might have felt, when going through some of its slow transitions from chaos into habitable earth, — waiting for sunshine, and bursting buds, and running rivers. I suppose I am not ready for full life yet.

December 16. To-day there are rumors of a possible war with England, on account of the affair of Mason and Slidell, now prisoners in Boston harbor.

It will be an outrage on humanity, a proof that England's pompous declamations against slavery are all hypocritical, if this should be done; for all good authorities have declared that a war on this account would never be, unless a pretext for war was wanted. Perhaps Providence intends that this shall be brought out definitely as a struggle for principles; I think the nation and the army need some such lesson, and they will not learn it unless it is made very plain.

December 22. I have found what are to be my two books of Bible study, — my two Sabbath books for the term. They are Neander's "History of the Church," and Conybeare and Howson's "Life of St. Paul." I have commenced them both, and find that satisfaction in them that is only met with by coming in contact with a character, — gifted, scholarly and Christian.

How I should like to live a free life with nature one year through! out in the bracing winds, the keen frosty air, and over the crackling snowcrust, wherever I would; and then in summer, seek the mountains or the sea, as I chose; no study, no thoughts, but what came as a thing of course; no system, except nature's wild ways, which have always their own harmony, evident enough when one enters into them, though understood by no mere observer.

December 28. A pretty table found its way into my room Christmas morning, a gift contributed from two classes; I was half sorry and half glad to receive it; I don't think I appreciate this kind of a present — it represents so many persons, some vaguely and some clearly fixed in memory — so much as a simpler token from the heart of one friend. And yet I feel the kindness which prompted the gift, and am grateful for it, I am sure.

How ashamed one is obliged to be just now of the "mother country"! *Step-mother Country* England ought to be called, for her treatment of us in our trouble. It is hard to believe that all she has said against slavery was insincere, and that she would really like to see the slave-power established and flourishing on the ruins of our free Republic; but her actions say so.

Yet we are not guiltless; not wholly purged from the curse yet. The army is not entirely anti-slavery in principles; and we cannot look for success, nor wish it, but for the sake of freedom.

CHAPTER VI.

INTELLECTUAL EXPERIENCES.

JANUARY 19, 1862. How hard it is to know anything of history, to learn enough to feel at all competent to teach! I said I would look through Gibbon, but I had hardly reached the times of Julian, before my class must be hurrying beyond Charlemagne, and I must turn to French histories to help them along. Then, between de Bonnechose and Sir James Stephen, with the various writers on the Middle Ages, which must be consulted for the history of the feudal system, free cities, and the Papacy, comes in the remembrance of my Bible class in the early history of the church, and I must give some hours to Neander! Meanwhile, another class is reading Shakespeare, and I want them to be somewhat critical, and must therefore read, myself; while yet another class in Metaphysics are beginning the history of philosophy, and I want them to know something about Plato, and the Alexandrian schools, and knowing very little myself I must find out something first. So I bring to my room the volumes containing the "Timæus" and the "Republic;" but in the midst of it, I remember that there are some compositions to be corrected, that I may be ready for the new ones Monday morning.

This is pretty much where Saturday night finds me, and so the weeks go on, this winter. I am glad to be busy, but I dislike to be superficial. Now, if I could teach only history, I should feel as though I might hope to do something. Girls will be ill-educated, until their teachers are allowed the time and thought which teachers of men are expected to take.

January 22. I am trying to get an idea which is rolling in grand chaos through my mind into shape for a composition theme for my first class this afternoon. It is the power of the soul in moulding form, — from the great Soul of the universe, down to lower natures, — down to animal and vegetable life. Plato's doctrine of ideas is the only starting-point I can think of; some thoughts of Swedenborg's will help; then Lavater and the Physiologists and Psychologists. But I want them to use it practically; to take particular persons, features, shape, gait, manner, voice, life; and then observe closely how beauty develops itself in flowers, leaves, pebbles, into infinite variety, yet according to invariable laws. It is a hard thing to bring such subjects into shape which young girls can grasp; yet they are the best things for opening the mind upon a broad horizon.

For a review of the week I must think of Plato; the "Republic," and "Timæus," and "Critias," I have succeeded in looking through; I have heard my "Mental" class read some of the rest. In the "Republic," I remember it is decided that youths should be taught in music, — no enfeebling melodies, but those which strengthen and build up the soul in all that is vast and true. Plato's idea of music comprehends more than we read in the word; and I see how it is that an education should be musical, — the spiritual fabric rising like the walls of Troy to the Orphean strains of noble thoughts and impulses.

I remember, too, that he would forbid some of the stories of the Gods to be told to children; those which should needlessly alarm them, or weaken their reverence. In that corrupt and yet beautiful system, it was necessary indeed; the same idea might be not injuriously carried out in a system of Christian education. In the Hebrew Scriptures there is much that puzzles the maturest minds, sincere and earnest in their search for truth; yet these narratives are the first knowledge that children often have of the Bible. I would have them learn only the New Testament, until they have learned something of the real nature of the world they are ushered into. When they study other history, they will be better able to understand this; and the history of the Jews is, it seems to me, a wonderful part of the world's record, so connected with that of other nations as to make them plainer, revealing the handwriting of an Almighty Providence everywhere.

I would not have the child begin life with the terror which hung over my childhood: told that I was a sinner before I knew what sin meant, and fearful pictures of eternal punishment which awaited all sinners at death haunting my dreams, so that I was afraid to sleep, and more afraid to die. I know they say (a good man has just said it to me) that there is less vigor of mind and character because these things are less taught as a part of religion than formerly; yet I am sure that blind fear cannot invigorate, — it must degrade. I believe that I went far down from my earliest ideals of life after hearing these things; and it was a long straying amid shadowy half-truths, and glooms of doubt, and stagnations of indifference, before I came back to the first thought of my childhood. No: let a child's life be beautiful as God meant it to be, by keeping it near Him, by showing to its simplicity the things which are lovely, and true, and pure, and of good report. The knowledge of evil comes rapidly enough, in the petty experiences of life; but a child will soon love evil and grow old in it, if driven away from the divine light of love; if not allowed to think of God chiefly as a friend. And just here is where Christ speaks to the hearts of little children; they know Him as soon as He is permitted to speak, and are known of Him.

January 29. I believe that letter-writing is more of a reality to me now than conversation; short though my notes are, I can speak thus to those who need me, and whom I need.

Repose of character, and the power of forgetting, are great compensations for a tried, hurried, and worried life. And there is, in all but the most unusual lives, something like this, which enables people to laugh at care, and triumph over grief; though it is never perfectly done, except by a thorough trust in the goodness of God, — a faith in the watching love.

February 5. I did have the sleigh-ride with my young friends, as I expected, and a merry one it was. We just whirled through Attleboro, and back again. All I remember of the ride is the icicles that hung on the orchard trees and, just at sunset, the tints that fell on a slope of unstained snow. They were the softest, coolest shades of blue and violet, with here and there a suggestion of rose or crimson, a perfectly magical combination of shadow colors, only half escaped from their white light-prison of the snow. It was a hint of the beauty of an Alpine or a Polar landscape, such as travelers tell about. The young moon followed one queenly star down the west, as we returned, with a song of "Glory Hallelujah," and "Homeward Bound."

February 6. The clear blue of this morning's sky has melted into a mass of snowy clouds, and now earth and sky are of the same hue, — white — white, — the purest crystalline snow is on the ground, and more is coming. The violet hues in the north at sunrise and sunset are very beautiful.

I am glad I took my walk in the woods this morning while the sky was bright; there are fine tints there always on the trees, various browns of withered oaks and beech-leaves, still persistent, and leaning against the stout pine trunks, that hold up their constant green to the sky. Two trees I noticed for the first time, a pine and a maple, which have grown up with their trunks in close union, almost one from infancy. One keeps his dark green mantle on, the other has lost her light summer robe, but is covered all over with the softest clinging lichens, that contrast their pale green tints with the white-gray bark in a charming way. When snow falls on these lichen-draped boughs, the softness of the white above and the white below is wonderful. I think Neck-woods is a grand studio; when weary of my own white walls I can always find refreshment there.

February 7. The news of Sarah Paine's death overwhelms me, — so young, so sensitive, so genial and accomplished; she seemed made to enter deeply into the reality and beauty of an earthly life. No pupil of mine has ever yet come near me in so many ways to sympathize and gladden as she. Only a few weeks since, we walked together in the woods, so full of life and hope she was; and now, in a moment, — but why this sorrow, since she is but suddenly called home to deeper love and purer life?

How every failure of tenderness and perfect appreciation on my part comes back to pain me now! Why have I not written to her? Why have I waited for her to write to me? Oh, what is worse than to fail of loving truly?

February 13. I had decided to go to her funeral, and went to Boston for the purpose, but a sleepless night left me too wretched to undertake the journey, and I spent the days in Boston feeling too miserable to come back here, or to stay there. How much of my life is gone with this friend! — gone? no; translated, lifted up with her to her new estate! Yet much *is* gone from the world: the beauty of the walks about here, of the studies we have loved and pursued together, — I hardly knew how much this young life had woven itself into mine. And it was the deeper, spiritual sympathies fusing all love into one deep harmony of life, — it was the love of the all-loving One that brought us closest together; and that makes "*was*" the wrong word to use, in speaking of her; she *is* my friend still, and the light of her new life will enter into mine.

One after another, those who have come nearest to me to love, to sympathize, to guide, pass on into purer air, and make me feel that my life is not here; my *home* is with the beloved.

February 17. There is news to-day of great victories in progress for us. Fort Donelson is surrounded; there has been a deadly fight, and our flag waves upon the outer fortifications. It is said that the rebels must yield, as all approaches are cut off, but it is the struggle of desperation with them, as this is the key to the whole Southwest. There are victories in Missouri and in North Carolina also; more prisoners taken than our generals know what to do with; but all this is purchased at *such* a price of blood!

In the days I stayed in Boston last week I visited two galleries of paintings, ancient and modern. The old paintings are chiefly curious, not beautiful, often very coarse in conception. I should like to see something really great by the "old masters;" but I suppose such things are only to be seen in Europe.

I believe I love landscape more than figures, unless these latter are touched by a master's hand. To be commonplace in dealing with nature does not seem quite so bad as in dealing with human beings.

I heard Ralph Waldo Emerson speak too. "Civilization" was his subject; nobly treated, except that the part of Hamlet was left out of Hamlet. What is civilization without Christianity? There was a kind of religion in what he said; an acknowledging of all those elements which are the result of Christianity; indeed, Emerson's life and character are such as Christianity would shape. He only refuses to call his inspiration by its right name. The source of all great and good thought is in Christ; so I could listen to the Sage of Concord, and recognize the voice of the Master he will not own in words.

"*Hitch* your wagon to a star!" was his way of telling his hearers to live nobly, according to the high principles which are at the heart of all life. The easiest way to live, he said, was to follow the order of the Universe. So it is. "The stars in their courses fought against Sisera;" but it was because Sisera would go the opposite way to the stars. This is the secret of our struggle, and of our victory that will be. We have entangled ourselves with wrong, have gone contrary to the Divine Order; now, if we come out plainly and strongly on the right side, we triumph; for Right cannot fail. This war will make a nation of great and true souls; if we fight for freedom. And what else is worth the conflict, the loss of life? The Union, a Country — a home? Yes, if these may be preserved in honor and humanity, not otherwise. Better be parceled out among the nations than keep the stigma of inhumanity upon our great domain. Freedom for slavery is no freedom to a noble soul.

February 21. I have often wondered what is the meaning of these dim forebodings, that, without any apparent cause, will sometimes make us so uneasy. The air is bright, cold, and clear; everything without says, "Rejoice and be strong!" everything within is darkened by vague, unaccountable flutterings of anticipated ill. No sorrow can come to *me* which will not involve some greater grief of other hearts, so I dread the more what I have to dread. I think I cannot say of anything that is dear to me, that it is all my own; can any one? Mothers, lovers, husbands, wives — these have exclusive joys, and exclusive losses to risk. I can lose much, for I love much; yet there is nothing on earth that I can feel myself holding firmly as mine. So I seek to live in others' joy and sorrow.

A life large and deep in its love, is the privilege of those placed as I am; it must be either that, or quite unloving, shut up in its own small case of selfishness. "When Thou shalt enlarge my heart," this large feeling of rest will be found.

I have plans floating in my mind for the education of my nieces. I could not afford to have them *here* without a salary much increased.

I think I could conduct their education myself, in some small school, better than here, more according to my own ideas; whether that is really better or not, only the results would show. But some of their studies I know I could make more valuable to them than those to whom they might be trusted. Then I have an idea of moral, religious, and mental development going on at the same time, which I do not often see carried out; perhaps I should not do it, but I should like to try. Having no children of my own I feel a responsibility for those who are nearest me. How much of an effort one should make for such a purpose as this, I do not know. So far, I have been evidently *led* into the way I ought to take; may it be so still!

It was a new sight to me, to see a long line of cavalry, extending far out of sight down the street, a forest of bayonets at first, and then an army of horses. It was our National Guard; and it looked like a strong defense, that bristling line of bayonets; but it made me very sad to think that men must leave home, and peaceful occupations, and moral influences, to punish rebellious brethren, and keep them in awe. War, as a business, is one that I cannot learn to believe in, although I must realize it as a necessity.

February 26. For any of us to comprehend thoroughly Kant, Fichte, Schelling, Hegel — to say nothing of the plainer sensualistic systems — in the little time we can give to the study, is quite out of the question. And yet it does these young girls good to know that there is a region of thought above and beyond their daily track, and if they should ever have time, they may enjoy exploring it. Besides, the habit of looking upon life in a large way comes through philosophy Christianized. The right use of our faculties in a reverent search for truth is certainly worth much thought and painstaking from man or woman.

To live a child-like, religious life in all things is what I would do; simply receiving light and life from the love revealed within, and so, as a child, claiming the inheritance of the world without, which was created by the same Love for loving souls; but the earthly cleaves to me; I lose simplicity of soul in the world's windings.

Yet I own but one Life, one Lord and Redeemer; in Him only shall I find for myself the simplicity of the child and the wisdom of the Seraph. In Him all things are mine. Beautiful ideals may deceive one. Because we see and can talk about noble things, does it follow that we can live them? I fear not always.

March 5. My birthday, — and I am as much

gratified as any child to find fragrant and beautiful flowers in my room, placed there by loving hands. And, what was very beautiful to me, the trim-berry vine which I have kept in a dish of moss all winter, this morning put forth one hesitating, snow white blossom, another followed before noon, and to-night there are four, as delicate in perfume as in color; it is so sweet, that the woods give me this pretty memento of their love to-day; it is a promise of spring, too; of the multitudes of just such white blossoms that are waiting patiently under the snow-banks to give themselves away in beauty and fragrance by and by. — To-night, for the first time, I met some of our scholars to talk with them of deep and sacred truths. I hardly know how I did it; it seemed hard at first, and yet it *was* easy, for the words seemed to be spoken through me. I will try not to shrink from it again. And I will endeavor to keep it before myself and others, that Christianity is simply a receiving and living out the life of Christ; not a thing of theories and emotions, but a *life*.

I will say it to these pages, because I feel it so bitterly sometimes, and cannot speak it out here without offense, that there is too much of the "tearing open of the rosebud" in talking with those who are seeking the truth. Some are thought to be indifferent or untrue, because they will not speak of their deepest feelings to anybody who asks them. It is a shameful mistake; it must accompany a low standard of delicacy, to say the least. Let me not call that pride or obstinacy, which is the heart's natural reserve! The deeper depths of the soul are sacred to one Eye alone, and so much as a shrinking soul may reveal to a friend, it will. I would discourage too free a conversation about one's own feelings; it is dissipating, except where a burdened soul *must* pour out itself to another for sympathy. Why cannot we leave our friends to find God in the silence of the soul, since there is His abode?

March 11. We have had victories by sea and land. To-night the news comes that Manassas is occupied by our troops. The "Merrimac" has made a dash from Norfolk, and destroyed two of our war vessels; but the little iron-clad "Monitor" appeared and drove her back. The coast of Florida is forsaken by the rebels, and our troops are taking possession. Everything is working for us now; and it seems as if the rebellion must soon be strangled. Sometimes it seems to me as if these events were happening in a foreign country, they touch me and mine so little in a way that we immediately feel.

This has been a day of "clearing up," and domestic reforms are never poetical. Taking down pictures and books, and finding one's self reminded of neglected favorites by heaps of dust, lost mementos coming up from forgotten corners, — after all, there is some sentiment in it; and, in the midst of it, three letters, two of them touching my heartstrings right powerfully.

I have learned to live with a trusting heart and a willing hand from day to day, and I have not a wish for more, except that I might be able to help others as I am not now able. If it is rest that is before me, I dare not take it until I am more weary than now; — a *home* would withdraw me from the opportunity of educating my nieces, perhaps. No! there can be nothing but single-handed work for others before me; anything else would be but a temptation, and perhaps one that I should not be able to bear. I would be kept safe from everything but a plain opening to the life of self-sacrifice in the footsteps of our one true Guide! I will trust Him for all, and be at rest from the dread of too much sunshine, as well as from fear of storms. He knows what I need.

There is heart-heaviness for souls astray, such as I have seldom felt, weighing me down even now. There is one poor girl, half ruined, and not knowing how to escape destruction, for whom there seems no outlet but into the very jaws of death. None but a Divine Power can help her; yet He may do it by making human helpers appear for her. How fearful a thing it is to be placed where there are brands to be plucked from burning.

And this is not the only one I know, for whom all human efforts *seem* unavailing. Near and far away are those to whom my heart reaches out with nameless fears, and hope unquenched and unquenchable, till the lamp of life shall go out. God save us all from shipwreck of soul! for these drifting lives but show us the possibilities of our own.

With poor little Prince Arthur, I can sometimes

say heartily, "Would I were out of prison, and kept sheep."

One long summer all out of doors, what new life it would give me! Yet I would not have this winter's memory left out of my life for much. Some new openings into true life, here and beyond, come with every season.

March 16. I have been trying to hold some plain converse with myself, and I am more and more convinced that sincerity is not the thorough spirit of my life, as I would have it. It is so easy to take one's fine theories, and the frequent expression of them, in the place of the realities they stand for. I really fear that I have been trying to impose these fine theories upon Him who knows my heart, in the place of true love. I believe in self-forgetfulness, in constant thought for others, in humility, in following the light of the unseen Presence within the soul, but I do not live out these ideas, except in languid and faltering efforts.

Now in this way, is not my life going to be a false one, false to man and God? Discouraging indeed it is, to think much of self; and it is well that we need not do it. There is life, there is truth to be had for the asking. Only the Christ-life within can make me true before heaven and earth and my own heart. Yet even here I feel myself so apt to dwell upon the beautiful theory of a present Redeemer as to forget that in the trifles of a daily intercourse with human beings, this life is to be manifested, if at all. Thoroughly unselfish — shall I ever be that?

I was glad to talk with my Bible scholars about the resurrection to-day. It has come to be the most real of all revealed truths to me.

Our Lord is risen, and we have a Redeemer to stand by our souls in the struggles of this human life. He is risen, and we shall arise from the dead, and go home to Him, "and so be forever with the Lord." He is risen, and all His and our beloved are risen with Him; they are "alive from the dead forevermore." He is risen, and we rise with Him from the death of sin, into the new life of holiness which he has brought into the world. He said, "Because I live, ye shall live also."

Beverly, April 5. Two, almost three, weeks of the vacation are gone. It is Saturday night, and after a week of fine spring weather, there is another driving snowstorm, which makes us all anxious, as our good brother Isaac has just sailed from Boston; but perhaps he is at anchor in the Roads; they would not start with the signs of a northeast storm at hand. Bound for Sumatra, to be gone a year, perhaps two. How we shall all miss him! He is one of the really kind-hearted, genial men, who know how to make home and friends happy, just by being what they are; no effort, no show about it, genuine goodness of heart making itself always felt.

I have had a week of visiting, also. Curious contrasts one finds, in passing from family to family; each has its own peculiar essence or flavor, its home element, or lack of the same; sometimes its painful peculiarity, which it seems almost dishonorable for a guest to notice, or ever even to think of, afterwards. One thing is plain, — the worldly-prosperous learn with most difficulty the secret of home-rest; whoever loves show has not the true home-love in him.

Those are the happiest family circles which are bound together by intangible, spiritual ties, in the midst of care, poverty, and hard work, it may be. Whether rich or poor, a home is not a home unless the roots of love are ever striking deeper through the crust of the earthly and the conventional, into the very realities of being, — not consciously always; seldom, perhaps; the simplicity of loving grows by living simply near nature and God.

And I have looked into some pleasant homes during this brief visit. Homes where little children are, are always beautiful to me, for the children's sake, if for nothing more. Cherub-like or impish, the little folks fascinate me always. If I were a mother, I am afraid I should never want my baby to grow up; and who knows whether the babies that die do not keep the charm of infancy upon them forever? So many little children I have loved have gone home with tiny life-torches just filling some small domestic world with light, a light that could not go out, and which perhaps heaven needs to make it perfect heaven.

But the best visit of all is always to Amesbury, to the friendly poet, and my loving Lizzie, his sister; dearer and dearer she seems to me, now so alone, without her mother. Since Esther went away, my longing love goes after this friend, my own Elizabeth, as if, when Heaven opened to receive one friend, a golden cord were flung down to us two, to bring us nearer each other and nearer the beloved ones up there. But theirs is a home in each other's love which makes earth a place to cling to for its beauty yet. If I could not think of them together there, of the quiet light which bathes everything within and around their cottage under the shadow of the hill, of the care repaid by gentle trust, of the dependence so blessed in its shelter of tenderness and strength, the world would seem to me a much drearier place; for I have never seen anything like this brother's and sister's love, and the home-atmosphere it creates, the trust in human goodness and the Divine Love it diffuses into all who enter the charmed circle.

I love to sit with my friends in the still Quaker worship; there is something very soothing in the silence of the place to me, and in glancing upon the faces around me, where "the dove of peace sits brooding." Then and there, I have often felt the union of all hearts in the truth, where there is no thought of opinion, or sect, or creed, but the one wide communion of trust in one Father and Redeemer which is His church; the gathering of all souls in Him.

April 17. I feel better prepared to write than I ever have, and I feel a greater desire to say what I am able to say, if I may. I do not know what my greatest use in life is yet, whether I can do more by teaching or by writing; I wait to be shown and to be guided, and I believe I shall be.

April 22. . . . The best preparation for death is to be alive as fully as one is capable of being; for the transition is not from life to death, but from life to life; *more* life always. And the time when we are to be called hence need not trouble us, or the way: it is in the heart of the Father to do the best thing for us forever.

May 4. I have been to Esther's grave, and found Spring there, a glimpse of the immortal sunshine and blossoming in which she lives. I have found love growing for me in her home, in one young, glad heart; and in one life-worn and sorrow-worn. I have felt *her* spirit living and breathing yet in her earthly home; from her flowers, her books, her domestic life, in all the atmosphere of the places haunted by her footsteps, — the home where she lived and loved and suffered, the lovely resting-place of her dust by the river side. Of such lives as hers new life is born, and I have brought back with me a deeper reality to live in, heaven bends nearer over me, earth is lifted up to heaven. I only needed to breathe in another, freer atmosphere than this; and the dear Lord sent me just where it was best for me to go. Scarcely could I have found anything so good for my soul's health, this side of the "fields beyond the swelling flood," where Esther, my heart's sister, walks with the Angels in the bloom of immortal health and loveliness.

It is strange, but I seem to know her more *humanly* now than when she was here. I saw her but once or twice; she was to me as a spirit, a voice in the wilderness, to guide and to cheer. Now I feel how she wore the same robes of flesh, wearily and painfully, yet cheering and blessing household and friends by her patient, tender love. I never thought before how beautiful it would be to visit the Holy Land — to tread in the Lord's footsteps. I had thought that the spirit-love might be dimmed by traces of the earthly; but it is not so; I have tracked the footsteps of this loving pilgrim through the Gethsemane and Olivet of her Holy Land of home, and I know her and hers more truly; I am hers, and she is mine more surely now forever.

May 10. Heaven is a *place*, a home, a rest: but it is a Spiritual habitation, Truth and Love and Peace are the pillars that support it; and it is the truthful, the loving, and the holy only who may enter in. How then, O beloved Guide, may such as I? Because Thou hast drawn me by love to Love, — hast given an "earnest" of that life even here, imparting new sympathies, hopes, and aspirations, infusing Thine own life into mine, and Thou wilt never forsake Thine own work, Thine own home! Yet so imperfectly I hear and follow Thee, so slow, so cold, so hard my nature yet, — when the summons comes, will it not find me lagging on the heavenly road, hardly at home within the beautiful gates? So many die with noble purposes half-grown into achievement, so many live but half in the light, and yet the Light is in them, — how will it be with them, and with me; how shall the stains of the mortal be put off? Death has no cleansing power, and defilement may not enter heaven. There is a mystery here which is too painful; yet we know not what that other life is, nor how hereafter, more than here, the Shepherd leads His own.

Always it is by paths they have not known; and what new and wonderful ministries may be prepared for us there, who have sought Him through all our faltering and waywardness here, He knows; and it is good to trust Him always, and for all things.

Sabbath, May 11. Esther's letters are a constant comfort to me; they say more to me now, about some things, than they did while she was alive. I love to keep them near me — in sight. Does she know how happy she makes me every day I live, how rich I am in the inheritance of love she has left me? Ah! how little can I tell what she is doing for me now! But the "idea of her life" seems growing into all my thoughts. I could not have known her as I do if she had not gone away, to return in spirit; and I can see her, too, moulding the lives of others she loved most dearly. There is more of heaven in this Spring's sunshine than I have seen for years.

I owe my acquaintance with Robertson to her; a gift she sent me out of deepest pain, when she was passing through the fires, and none but Jesus knew. I use his thoughts on the epistle to the Corinthians with my class these Sunday mornings; that is, I read the Apostle's words, then Robertson's, then the Apostle's again, and afterward talk with the scholars from the things which I have, in both ways, received. And by the kindling eyes and earnest looks of all, especially of some whose natures have seemed indolent and unspiritual, I feel assured that the living thought is sometimes found and received mutually. A soul must drink the truth, bathe in it, glow with its life, in order to impart it to another soul; and it is to me a source of gratitude which I can never exhaust, that such as Robertson and my Esther "have lived and died."

May 13. Yesterday morning the news came of the surrender of Norfolk, and, in a sudden burst of patriotism, the school went out and marched round the Liberty pole, under the Stars and Stripes, singing "Hail Columbia," and cheering most heartily.

The defeat of the rebels — happily bloodless — was attended with the usual amount of vandalism, burning of buildings, ships, etc. The stolen ship "Merrimac," transformed into an iron-fanged rebel war steamer, was blown up; we are all glad her race is run. And the vandalism of the rebels is but another proof to the world of the worth of their cause, the desperate situation in which they find themselves, and on which side of the contest barbarism lingers. All hearts are lighter now. The doom of this demoniac rebellion is sealed. There is no longer any slavery in the District of Columbia, and doubtless the whole infamous "system" shall be drowned out in the blood of this war. If not, it will seem to have been shed in vain.

May 21. C—— has gone into the army; but first he has "joined the army of the Lord," as he expresses it in his letter to his mother. If ever mortals could hear the angels rejoicing "over one that repenteth," I should think I had heard them to-day, while I read this news. So much anxiety lest here should be a shipwrecked soul, so many have been pained about him, and burdened for him, — so little faith or hope some of us had, as to the possibility of his rising out of his old self into a better life, — all these memories come back, and make it seem like a miracle; and indeed it is the greatest of all miracles.

And when he writes, "Aunt Lucy may feel as if her prayers were being answered," it seems to me as if I had nothing but unbelief to remember. It is the mighty hand of God, if he is saved! He goes into temptation, but he goes hopeful, and longing to prove himself a "good soldier of the Cross." And now he needs to be followed with faith and prayer more than ever. It seems to me as if this were realizing for the first time, what "conversion" means; that it is a reality, and not a term which custom has made mere cant. He speaks of himself in a free, simple way, as *I* never could have spoken; and yet it *is* genuine. Oh, if it might unloose more hearts and tongues!

May 23. . . . I am so glad to be *needed*, as I

seem to be now, by several of my friends: my thoughts, my care, my suggestions seem of some value. It is a woman's want, and I feel a woman's gratification in being allowed to think a little for others. For a great school like this, I never feel that I can do much; I want to know just the especial need of somebody that I can help.

So human nature goes: absorbed by petty miseries quite as much as by grand and beautiful ideas; who would think, sometimes, that such as we could be immortal beings?

I have felt myself growing very skeptical for a little while, of late. A cold thrill creeps insidiously through me when I go among people; there is so little apparent reality in human lives, loves, friendships. "All seek their own;" and when there is a gleam of unselfishness, it is but a passing gleam. And, worst of all, when I am with those whose lives are pitched in a low key, I find myself taking it for granted that it is life.

June 7. Two trials came to me this week, trials to patience which I seldom have, yet both very trifling. One came from a selfish woman, who *would* misunderstand me, and imagine that I was troubling her, when I was trying to do just the opposite; this I must bear in silence, for it is a case when doing and letting alone are accounted alike grievous. Another was from the whims of school-girls, which they would persevere in, though to their own serious discomfort. How to meet such things with simple meekness, and not with a desire to let people suffer the consequences of their own mistakes, is something, which, old as I am, I have not yet learned. The constant frets of this kind that some have to bear, I have been saved from; people are generally too generous and thoughtful of me. How miserable some families must be! and what a wretched life it must be, just to be left to the indulgence of one's own foolish and selfish whims!

June 11. This week I wrote letters which decide my going to Connecticut, to Esther's mother, next year. It is strange that it seemed so hard for me to decide upon so pleasant a thing; but somehow it is as if this were altogether a different thing from my usual plans; as if there were hidden links in spiritual chains influencing my decision, and to result from it. I do not know whether I have decided right, but I believe some good will come out of it, in some way. If I can make a desolate home a little happier, it will be worth going for; but that is just the thing I fear I shall not do.

June 22. . . . I was most wretchedly tried, today, by a bungler in dentistry, and then worried and vexed by two hours' hurried and dissatisfied shopping.

. . . I know that I am loved and valued here, and yet I want to go away. I do not think of any place where I long to go, but only somewhere into a different life: into more trials I am sure it will be, when I do go, but that does not frighten me. I am growing callous with the constant repetition of the same blessings. I need to suffer, to be shaken sorely through all my life, then perhaps I shall learn not to be so ungrateful or indifferent to anything God sends.

July 9. If Atlas had undertaken to keep a journal of his state of mind, while holding the world on his shoulders, he might have been successful and he might not; and it might or might not have been worth while. I don't want to "keep a journal" exactly, but I want to try the effect of writing every day, as much to keep up the habit as anything else. But how to catch the moments from between the busy hours? I am to be here another anniversary, — no help for it, though greatly against my wishes: the work that comes with it does not seem to me very profitable to anybody in particular, and the hardest of it comes upon me. I dislike shows and preparation for shows; but there is no escaping. There is an interest in helping the girls do their parts well, only they and I both fear I help them too much sometimes.

. . . At night a most kind letter from my editor friend with a most liberal enclosure for services rendered. The nobleness and genial spirit of the man is more to me even than his liberality. It is a comfort to write for those who receive in the spirit of one's giving.

And to-day a letter from a young nephew, confiding to me his longings for a better life, and asking for suggestions and advice. This is a joy that brought tears to my eyes; not that I can do much for him, except by helping him to keep those aspirations alive; by sympathy and by living such a life as he seeks. It is like a miracle, in these days, when a young man like him really is interested in such things! An upright, moral one too, with few bad habits, and the promise of a successful worldly career.

Beverly, last of July. The war moves on, but slowly. The "rallying" meetings to raise the President three hundred thousand men seem like an attempt at galvanizing patriotism into life. Blindness is come upon the people in some way, for some reason: it is not as in the old Revolutionary days; and yet this cause is greater. But we will not dare to say that we are fighting for anything but the Government. We leave God out, and all becomes confused.

July 29. Another death; C——, the stray lamb so long, has been called into the upper fold. His was a wonderful change, as marked as St. Paul's, almost, and his last letter from the camp was one that will be a lifelong comfort to his friends, so full of faith in God, submission to His will, an entire readiness to die, and yet a wish to live that the past might be redeemed. He died on the 25th of June, while his division of the army was passing from Corinth to Memphis, after having suffered much from fever, and other complaints incident to a weakened constitution in a new climate, and among the hardships of war. He had his wish; his long desire to be a soldier was gratified; once he was under fire; the air full of bullets around him, and one striking within two feet of his head. But he was not to die in battle; disease, that he dreaded more, laid him low; he longed for civilization, was weary of the great Southern forests; but there he was to lay his weary head for his last sleep. And now his mother is all alone in the world, and almost broken-hearted. One after another, husband and four children have gone, and she is a widow and childless.

But to think of the thousands of homes that this war has desolated, the thousands of hearts well-nigh broken! Is it not enough?

No, for the purification of the nation has not yet been wrought out; the scourge is needed yet; the gulf yet yawns for that which is dearest in all the land, and the war will not cease until it is closed. Not to a proud, self-confident people will the victory be given, but to the humble, the trustful, the nation that stays itself upon God, and lives only for the highest principles, and the highest love.

August 10. This week has been a more remarkable one than any in my life, I believe, in the way of seeing people I have heard of, and had some little curiosity about. Last Thursday was spent at Andover, and one of the golden days it was. The day itself was one of shine and shadow just rightly blended; and the place, the well-known Hill of the students, was in its glory. After sitting awhile in church, where the learned Professors, Park, Phelps, and Stowe, sat in state (I wonder if Professors dread anniversaries and conspicuous positions as we boarding-school teachers do!) we went up the hill to accept an invitation to lunch with Mrs. Harriet Beecher Stowe. It was beautiful as a page from one of her own story books.

Mrs. Stowe herself I liked, and her house and garden were just such as an authoress like her ought to have. It all had what I imagine to be an English look, the old stone house, with its wild vines and trees brought into shape in picturesque walks, and its cool refreshment-room looking off over the river, the city, and the far hills, to the mountains; the arrangement of the table, too, showing so much of the poetess. I could not have called upon Mrs. Stowe formally; as it was, nothing could have been much pleasanter, of that kind.

Then before I left I called upon some old friends; a call which finished the day very delightfully; for there, besides the cordiality of really well-bred people, I saw one of the sweetest specimens of girlhood that can be shown in New England, I fancy. Beauty does not often fascinate me, in its common acceptation; but where there is soul in a young, sweet face — modesty and intelligence that greet you like the fragrance of a rosebud before it is well opened — it is so rare a thing in these "Young America" days that it makes me a little extravagant in admiration, perhaps.

Saturday I spent at Amesbury; it was not quite like other visits, for two other visitors were there;

yet I enjoyed one of them especially; an educated mulatto girl, refined, lady-like in every respect, and a standing reply to those who talk of the "inferiority of the colored race." It is seldom that I see any one who attracts me so much, whose acquaintance I so much desire, just from first sight. She would like to teach at Port Royal, but the *government* will not permit. Ah, well! my book ends with no prospect of the war's end. Three hundred thousand recruits have just been raised, and as many more are to be drafted.

Many talk as if there never was a darker time than now. We have no unity of purpose; the watchword is "Fight for the Government!" but that is an abstraction the many cannot comprehend. If they would say, "Fight for Liberty — your own liberty, and that of every American," there would be an impetus given to the contest that, on our side, "drags its slow length along." This is an extreme opinion, our law-abiding people say, but I believe we shall come to worse extremes before the war ends.

CHAPTER VII.

LETTERS AND WORK.

1861–1868.

THE regular routine of school-life was varied for Miss Larcom by charming invitations to Boston where she met many literary friends, and by her pleasant summer vacations, which she always spent among the mountains. The two following letters, one to Mr. James T. Fields and one to Mr. Whittier, are interesting: —

NORTON, April 4, 1861.

DEAR MR. FIELDS, — My thoughts ran into a kind of rhapsody, all to themselves, after that evening of pleasant surprises at your house. I did not know it was fairy-land at 37 Charles Street, nor did I dream of meeting so many of the Genii, — if I had foredreamed or foreknown, I suppose I should have thought it even more of an impossibility for me to go than I did.

I was n't going to be so foolish as to send you this rhapsody, but I have just got back to my own room after the wanderings of vacation, and have hung up my ruined arch. It is Dolabella's, on the Cœlian Hill, and it brings back so many pleasant reminiscences of those few hours among the treasures of your home-grotto that I am just in the mood for inflicting this out-of-date expression of my enjoyment upon Mrs. Fields and you. I don't pretend that it is poetry, and if you are ashamed of me, for running on so, please remember that you should n't have shown me so many curious and beautiful things; — I am not used to them.

I have heard that Miss Cushman is to play next week. Is it true? If it is, and if you know beforehand what evenings she will appear as Lady Macbeth or Meg Merrilies, will you be so kind as to tell Mr. Robinson, who will let me know, and who has promised to accompany me to the theatre? I have always wanted to see her in some of her great *rôles*, and now more than ever, since I have seen her as a noble woman.

What a wonderful statue that "Lotus Eater" is! I was never so "carried away" with anything in marble!

With remembrances to Mrs. Fields,

Gratefully yours,

LUCY LARCOM.

This poem was enclosed in the above letter: —

Was it a dream
Or waking vision of the gracious night?
Did I on that enchanted isle alight,
Aye blossoming in Shakespeare's line,
With forms and melodies divine, —
Where all things seem
Ancient yet ever new beneath the hand
Of Prospero and his aërial band?

At every turn a change
To something rich and strange, —
Embodied shapes of poets' fantasies:
Glimpses of ruins old
Slow fading from the blue Italian skies;
And runes of wizards bold;
Or beautiful or quaint
Memorials of bard, and sage, and saint,
In many an antique tome.

There was some necromancy in the place:
The air was full of voices wondrous sweet;
Crowned shadows of past ages came to greet
Their living peers, who lately lent new grace
To genius-haunted Rome;
And when the lady of the grotto spoke,
'T was like Miranda, when at first she woke
To Love, lighting the wild sea with her smile
Star of her beautiful and haunted isle;
And the magician, who
Such harmony and beauty round him drew, —
He was her Ariel and Ferdinand
Blended in one,
And heir to Prosper's wonder-working wand.
He charmed the sprites of power
For one familiar hour,
And Story-land and Dream-land deftly won
To his home-nook the moonlit stream beside:
Hushed and apart
Though in the city's heart,
There dwell they long, the poet and his bride!

TO J. G. WHITTIER.

NORTON, MASS., September 8, 1861.

Why is it that I always miss thy visits? Why of all things should I have lost sight of thee at the mountains? and when I was so near thee too! I cannot think why so pleasant a thing should be withheld from me, unless because I enjoy it too much. I have no other such friends as thee and Elizabeth, and when anything like this happens it is a great disappointment. But I said all the time that seeing the hills with you could only be a beautiful dream.

I felt the beauty of those mountains around the Lake, as I floated among them, but I wished for thee all the while; because I have always associated thee with my first glimpse of them, and somehow it seems as if they belonged to thee or thee to them, or both. They would not speak to me much; I needed an interpreter: and when they grew so dim and spectral in the noon haze, they gave me a strange almost shuddering feeling of distance and loneliness.

But I am glad thee saw the Notch Mountains, and those grand blue hills up the river that I used to watch through all their changes. I am glad Miss B—— saw thee, for she was as much disappointed as I when we gave up the hope of your coming. I felt almost certain you would both come; I wanted Lizzie to know the mountains.

Is it right to dream and plan for another year? How I should like to go to Franconia with thee and Elizabeth to see those great gates of the Notch open gradually wider and wider, and then to pass through to a vision of the vast range beyond! It is but a vague memory to me; I long to take that journey again.

But everything has wearied me this summer,

and I feel almost like dropping my dreams and never expecting anything more. It is doubtless wiser to take what a kind Providence sends, just as it comes: yet who is always wise? Twice I rested in the sight of your beautiful river and on that cottage doorstep at Campton, looking off to the mountains. But the sea tired me with its restlessness. I wanted to tell it to be still. And I was very willing to get back from it to the quiet of my room, to the shelter of these friendly elms, and to the steady cheerful music of crickets and grasshoppers.

I shall be very happy to try to write a hymn for the Horticultural Association, as you request; and will send you something as soon as I can. . . .

In the autumn of 1862, Miss Larcom decided to give up teaching at Wheaton Seminary. Ill health for some time had made her complain of a constant sense of weariness in her head. Living in the crowded school when she longed for quiet, and preparing her work for extra classes, she became nervously exhausted; so that when an invitation came from Esther's mother, requesting her to spend the winter in Waterbury, Connecticut, she readily accepted it. She longed to be in the peaceful home made sacred by the presence of her beloved friend, where she felt that by occupying Esther's room, sitting at her writing-desk, and using her very bed, she would enter into her spirit, and help to fill the vacant place in a mother's heart. At first there was something hallowed in the home of one so pure, — she "felt it was holy ground," and was "half afraid to live my common life here;" but the close association with sad memories was depressing, and the solitude, while it gave her rest, did not refresh her. After having formed a lifelong friendship with Franklin Carter, a half-brother of Esther and afterwards President of Williams College, she returned, first to Norton for a little while, — then to Beverly, where she secured time for her writing, which was now constantly absorbing her attention.

Her poems, written chiefly for weekly papers — since they were either on homely fireside topics or incidents of the war, or else were religious meditations — were widely copied, and found their way into the scrap-books of thoughtful households all over the land. Referring to the winter of 1863, she said, "I have written for the newspapers this winter. My ideas of the 'Atlantic' are too high for me often to offer it anything my thoughts let slip. My standard is so far beyond my performances, that I am very glad to let them glide away unnoticed, and unnamed, on the path of the weekly tide wave of print." Though Mr. Fields was equal to the task of polite editorial refusal, he gladdened her heart by occasionally accepting a poem. It was through his literary judgment that "Hilary," that tender lyric of sea-sorrow, with its wistfulness and pathos, first saw the light; and the indignant strains of "A Loyal Woman's No" were first heard from the pages of the "Atlantic." These successes opened the way for poems of greater merit, like the "Rose Enthroned."

Her interest in the war was intense. She followed eagerly the progress of the campaigns, and rejoiced in every victory, often writing verses to celebrate the events, as in the case of the sinking Merrimac: —

"Gone down in the flood, and gone out in the flame!
What else could she do, with her fair Northern name?"

Her satire was ready for those able-bodied men who, when the drafting was talked of, were suddenly seized with many varieties of disease, or those who went a-fishing for the season — because mariners were exempt — or, like one man, who cut off three fingers, hoping that the loss of these members would be sufficient to keep him at home. She wanted to do something herself: "I am almost ashamed of these high sentiments in print, because I really have done nothing for our dear country as yet. These things sound conceited and arrogant to me, under the circumstances, but I only write from an ideal of patriotic womanhood, and for my country-women." She came near offering herself as a teacher for the "Contrabands," but some of her friends thought it unwise in the state of her health at the time, and she concluded that she was not fitted for the work, with the rather sad confession, "I have an unconquerable distrust of my own fitness for these angel ministries; I fear I am not worthy to suffer. I can think, write, and teach, but can I live?"

In August, 1863, she was called to the West by the serious illness of her sister Louisa, which terminated fatally.

TO MRS. JAMES T. FIELDS.

HAMMOND, WIS., September 11, 1863.

. . . and with her, my pleasant dreams of home dissolve; it was she who said she would make a home for me, wherever I would choose. The earthly outlook is lonelier than before; but I must not yield to selfish regrets. She has gone home, in a sense more real than we often say of the dead. Her whole family had gone before her, — husband and four children had left her one after another. Her heart seemed broken when her youngest son died in the army, last year; she never recovered her strength after that blow. I cannot mourn when I think of that glad reunion of a household in heaven, but I cannot help the great blank that her death and my brother's have left in my life. These family ties, I find, grow stronger as I grow older.

This prairie life does not now attract me at all. A broad, grand world opens out on every side, but there is no choice in it. You might as well take one level road as another. . . .

With the death of this sister, in reality, did dissolve the "pleasant dreams of a home," for Miss Larcom never had a home of her own, though she longed for one, and used to delight in speaking of the possibility of having one. "I will build my long-planned home among the mountains," she used to say, "and my friends shall bivouac with me all summer." But her life was spent principally in boarding-houses, or in the homes of others. Her resources never permitted her to own the bed on which she slept; however, she did own an old wooden lounge, which was her only bed for years. But she made the best of it, in her usual way; "I like this old couch. I like to be independent of things; there is a charm in Bohemian life."

On her return to Beverly in 1864, she took a few pupils again, and spent a good deal of time in painting, — even weeds, for she "loved the very driest old stick that had a bit of lichen or moss on it." She exhausted her friend's libraries in reading, and received from Mrs. Fields a large valise filled with precious volumes, which she returned only after having read them all. "I like to be here in Beverly with my sister and the children. I think I am more human here than at school."

The following records were made with feeling in her diary.

April 10, 1865. Waked at five o'clock this morning, to hear bells ringing for the surrender of Lee's army; robins screaming, and guns booming from the fort. The war's "Finis;" Glory Hallelujah!

April 15. Starting for Boston, the bells began to toll. The President's assassination is the report. The morning papers confirm the truth. Sadness and indignation everywhere. The Rebellion has struck its most desperate blow, but the Nation moves calmly on.

April 19. The President's funeral. Every place of business closed. Services in all the churches. I went to the Old South, and heard a brief and indignant speech, which received the people's earnest response.

May 14, Sunday. Bells ringing for the capture of Jeff Davis.

In 1865, Miss Larcom became one of the editors of the new magazine for young people, "Our Young Folks," and retained this position until 1872, when "St. Nicholas" inherited the good-will and patronage of the earlier magazine. The orange-colored periodical bore her name, and those of Gail Hamilton and Trowbridge, and usually contained a ballad or prose sketch by her, or else she contributed some of the answers in the "Letter Box." Her work was performed with conscientiousness and good taste; her sympathy with child-life made her a valuable assistant in making the magazine popular. She was interested in its success: "'Our Young Folks' greatly delights grown people everywhere. I am very glad of an occasional criticism that offers a hint of an improvement. It must be made to distance all competitors in value, as it does in patronage."

To be in a position where she had the power to reject or accept hundreds of manuscripts sent for approval, interested her, but she had so much sympathy for the struggling author, that, contrary to the usual custom of the "Editorial Department," she often sent a personal note of explanation. She could not help laughing over the strange letters she received, though she usually answered them politely. One woman wrote, asking her advice as to the sale of three hundred barrels of apples. Musicians sent her music, requesting her to write words to suit. A young girl wrote that she was "young, poor, and orphaned," thus appealing to the editorial sympathies, and requested her to arbitrate concerning the merit of two poems, "The Angel Whisper" and "One of the Chosen," for some one had promised to give her five dollars and a new hat, if her own poem should be successful. Modesty was not always a virtue with these applicants. One wrote: "Editors, Sir and Madam, — I send you a palindrome, which you know is a curiosity. I saw a list, the other day, said to be the best in the language, but this excels them all, as it represents a complete idea of spiritual philosophy. I should like to open a school of ideas for children. I believe this would add to your subscription list." Another announced the strange theory, that "languages were originated with references to correspondence between the visible and invisible world." Another facetiously remarked, making application for a position, "Anything but to count money, for I have not had experience in this form of labor."

Miss Larcom published, in 1866, the valuable collection of extracts from religious writings, —

"Breathings of the Better Life." It was received with warm welcome, and reprinted in England, without, however, being accredited to the author. It contained the passages she had discovered in her reading of many books, to which she wanted to give a wider circulation among those who might not possess the volumes. This little book represents the development of her religious thought along deeply spiritual lines. Her favorite authors are represented, — Robertson, Bushnell, Tholuck, and now and then a little poem by George Herbert, Madame Guyon, or Mrs. Browning is given. The subjects treated are characteristic of her thought: "The Kingdom within the Soul," "The Way of Access," "Life Eternal," "Shadows cast over Other Lives," "The Bearing of the Cross," "The Fullness of Life," "The Illuminated Gateway," and "The Glory Beyond."

TO MR. J. T. FIELDS.

BEVERLY, MASS., May 20, 1866.

MY DEAR MR. FIELDS, — Before you escape for the summer, I want to bother you with a word or two about the "Breathings." I find that people are imagining I have been very industrious this winter, by the way they talk about my new book, which they suppose is something original. I don't want to give wrong impressions in that way, as the selections are more valuable on their own account than on mine.

When it is time to announce it, can it not be described as "a compilation of brief extracts in prose and verse, from favorite religious writers," or something to that effect. And must my name appear in full? The commonplace "Miss Larcom" I should like better than my usual staring alliteration; as less obtrusive, "L. L." is better still.

And please let the book be as inexpensive as possible, because it is my "little preach," and I want a large congregation of poor folks like myself. My object in preparing it will be defeated, if they cannot have it.

I don't calculate upon a "paper fractional" from it for myself, so you can leave that entirely out of consideration. It has been altogether a labor of love with me. I wanted the good people to know who their best instructors are. Robertson above all, who is the true apostle of this age, within the Church.

Yours sincerely,

LUCY LARCOM.

TO MRS. J. T. FIELDS.

BEVERLY, MASS., May 26, 1866.

DEAR ANNIE, — If I could only make you feel the difference in myself coming home through the apple-blooms last night, and going to Boston Wednesday morning, I think you would know that you had not lived in vain, for a few of the beautiful May-day hours. I bring such refreshment from you always! I wonder if you do not feel that something is gone out from you, or are you like the flowers, that find an infinite sweetness in their hearts, replacing constantly what they give away? So much I must say in love and gratitude, and you must pardon it, because it is sincere.

I have copied the rhyme note for you. If I did not feel so very "stingy" (it's the word!) about our Mr. Whittier's letters, I should give you the original, for I think it belongs to you almost as much as to me. But possession is nine tenths of the law, you know, and I am a real miser about the letters of a friend, — ashamed as I am to own it to one so generous to me as you are. . . .

The "rhyme note" mentioned was a delightful doggerel from Mr. Whittier.

AMESBURY, March 25, 1866.

Believe me, Lucy Larcom, it gives me real sorrow
That I cannot take my carpet-bag, and go to town to-morrow;
But I'm "Snow-bound," and cold on cold, like layers of an onion,
Have piled my back, and weighed me down, as with the pack of
Bunyan.

The north-east wind is damper, and the north-west wind is colder,
Or else the matter simply is that I am growing older;
And then, I dare not trust a moon seen over one's left shoulder
As I saw this, with slender horn caught in a west hill-pine,
As on a Stamboul minaret curves the Arch Impostor's sign.

So I must stay in Amesbury, and let you go your way,
And guess what colors greet your eyes, what shapes your steps
delay,
What pictured forms of heathen love, of god and goddess please you,
What idol graven images you bend your wicked knees to.

But why should I of evil dream, well knowing at your head goes
That flower of Christian womanhood, our dear good Anna Meadows!

She 'll be discreet, I 'm sure, although, once, in a fit romantic,
She flung the Doge's bridal ring, and married the "Atlantic;"
And spite of all appearances, like the woman in the shoe,
She 's got so many "Young Folks" now she don't know what to do.

But I must say, I think it strange that thee and Mrs. Spalding,
Whose lives with Calvin's five-barred creed have been so tightly
walled in,
Should quit your Puritanic homes, and take the pains to go
So far, with malice aforethought, to walk in a vain show!
Did Emmons hunt for pictures? was Jonathan Edwards peeping
Into the chambers of imagery with maids for Tammuz weeping?

Ah, well, the times are sadly changed, and I myself am feeling
The wicked world my Quaker coat from off my shoulders peeling;
God grant that, in the strange new sea of change wherein we swim,
We still may keep the good old plank of simple faith in Him!

P. S. My housekeeper 's got the "tissick," and gone away, and
Lizzie
Is at home for the vacation, with flounce and trimmings busy;
The snow lies white about us, the birds again are dumb,—
The lying blue-frocked rascals who told us Spring had come;
But in the woods of Folly-Mill the sweet May-flowers are making
All ready for the moment of Nature's glad awaking.

Come when they come; their welcome share:—except when at
the city,
For months I 've scarce seen womankind, save when, in sheerest
pity,
Gail Hamilton came up, beside my lonely hearth to sit,
And make the Winter evening glad with wisdom and with wit
And fancy, feeling but the spur and not the curbing bit,
Lending a womanly charm to what before was bachelor rudeness;—
The Lord reward her for an act of disinterested goodness!

And now, with love to Mrs. F., and Mrs. S. (God bless her!),
And hoping that my foolish rhyme may not prove a transgressor,
And wishing for your sake and mine, it wiser were and wittier,
I leave it, and subscribe myself, your old friend,

JOHN G. WHITTIER.

TO MRS. J. T. FIELDS.

BEVERLY, June 21, 1866.

DEAR ANNIE, — Here I am once more by the salt sea, and out of the beautiful retreat of the Shakers, where we said "Good-by."

"Aunt Mary" told me I might come again, and if it were not for the vision of that great dining-room, and the "two settings" of brethren and sisters, and the general wash-basin, I should almost be tempted to go also, and steep myself in that great quietness: only one would need a book now and then, and literature seems to be tabooed among them.

Mr. Whittier was much interested to hear of our adventures. I think I must have been eloquent about cider, for he said, "I wish I had some of it this minute," so earnestly that I wished I had my hand upon that invisible Shaker barrel. . . .

TO MRS. CELIA THAXTER.

BEVERLY, July 16, 1867.

MY DEAR FRIEND, — To think that yesterday I was among the Enchanted Isles, and to-day here, with only the warm murmur of the west wind among the elms! The glory of the day and the far eastern sea lingers with me yet. How I do thank you for those three bright days! The undercurrent of memory would have been too much but for your kindness.

I think I kept it well covered, but there was a

vast unrest in me, all those days. I seemed to myself wandering over the turfy slopes, and the rocks, and the sea, in search of a dream, a sweet, impalpable presence that ever eluded me. I never knew how fully dear Lizzie[1] filled my heart, until she was gone. Is it always so? But that Island is Lizzie to me, now. It was the refuge of her dreams, when she could not be there in reality. Her whole being seemed to blossom out into the immense spaces of the sea. I am glad that I have been there once again, and with only the dear brother, and you whom she loved and admired so much. For you *are* an enchantress. It is a great gift to attract and to *hold* as you can, and rare, even among women. To some it is a snare, but I do not believe it ever can be to you, because the large generosity of the sea was born into you. How can you help it, if your waves overblow with music, and all sorts of mysterious wealth upon others of us humans? I hope you beguiled our friend into a stay of more than the one day he spoke of. It was doing him so much good to be there, in that free and easy way; just the life he ought to lead for half the year, at least. I shall always use my meagre arts most earnestly to get him to the Island when you are there. There is such a difference in human atmospheres, you know; the petty, east-wind blighted inhabitants of towns are not good for the health of such as he. I esteem it one of the wonderful blessings of my life that he does not feel uncomfortable

[1] Elizabeth Whittier.

when I am about. With you, there is the added element of exhilaration, the rarest thing to receive, as one gets into years.

It is a sacred trust, the friendship of such a man.

TO MISS JEAN INGELOW.

BEVERLY, MASS., December 15, 1867.

MY DEAR MISS INGELOW, — It was very kind of you to write to me, and I can hardly tell you how much pleasure your letter gave me, in my at present lonely and unsettled life. I think a woman's life is necessarily lonely, if unsettled: the home-instinct lies so deep in us. But I have never had a real home since I was a little child. I have married sisters, with whom I stay, when my work allows it, but that is not like one's own place. I want a corner exclusively mine, in which to spin my own web and ravel it again, if I wish.

I wish I could learn to think my own thoughts in the thick of other people's lives, but I never could, and I am too old to begin now. However, there are compensations in all things, and I would not be out of reach of the happy children's voices, which echo round me, although they will break in upon me rather suddenly, sometimes.

You asked about the sea, — our sea. The coast here is not remarkable. Just here there is a deep, sunny harbor, that sheltered the second company of the Pilgrim settlers from the Mother-Country, more than two centuries ago. A little river, which has leave to be such only at the return of the tide, half clasps the town in its crooked arm, and makes many an opening of beauty twice a day, among the fields and under the hills. The harbor is so shut in by islands, it has the effect of a lake; and the tide comes up over the wide, weedy flats, with a gentle and gradual flow. There are never any dangerous "High Tides" here. But up the shore a mile or two, the islands drift away, and the sea opens gradually as we near the storm-beaten point of Cape Ann, where we can see nothing but the waves and the ships, between us and Great Britain. The granite cliffs grow higher towards the Cape, but their hollows are relieved by little thickets of intensely red wild roses, and later, by the purple twinkling asters and the golden-rod's embodied sunshine.

The east wind is bitter upon our coast. The wild rocks along the Cape are strewn with memories of shipwreck. Perhaps you remember Longfellow's "Wreck of the Hesperus." The "Reef of Norman's Woe" is at Cape Ann, ten miles or so from here. About the same distance out, there is a group of islands, — the Isles of Shoals, which are a favorite resort in the summer, and getting to be somewhat too fashionable, for their charm is the wildness which they reveal and allow. Dressed up people spoil nature, somehow; unintentionally, I suppose; but the human butterflies are better in their own *parterres*. At Appledore, one of the larger of these islands, I have spent many happy days with the sister of our poet Whittier, now passed to the eternal shores, — and the last summer was there again, without her, alas! I missed her so, even though her noble brother was there! Perhaps that only recalled the lost, lovely days too vividly. I have seldom loved any one as I loved her.

These islands are full of strange gorges and caverns, haunted with stories of pirate and ghost. The old-world romance seems to have floated to them. And there I first saw your English pimpernel. It came here with the Pilgrims, I suppose, as it is not a native. It is pleasant to meet with these emigrant flowers. Most of them are carefully tended in gardens, but some are healthily naturalized in the bleakest spots. I should so like to see the daisies — Chaucer's daisies — in their native fields; and the "yellow primrose," too. Neither of these grows readily in our gardens. I have seen them only as petted house-plants.

I recognize some of our wild flowers in your "Songs of Seven." By the way, Mr. Niles has sent me an illustrated copy of it, and what a gem it is! But I hardly know what are especially ours. Have you the tiny blue four-petaled "Houstonia Cœrulia"? — our first flower of spring, that and the rock-saxifrage! And is October in England gladdened with the heavenly azure of the fringed gentian? And does the climbing bitter-sweet hang its orange-colored fruit high in the deep green of the pine-trees, in the autumn? The most wonderful climber I ever saw was the trumpet-vine of the West. It grew on the banks of the Mississippi, climbing to the top of immense primeval trees, bursting out, there, into great red, clarion-like flowers. It seems literally to fix a foot in the trees as it climbs,—and it has an uncivilized way of pulling the shingles off the roofs of the houses over which it is trained. I am glad that violets are common property in the world. The prairies are blue with them. How at home they used to make me feel! for they are New England blossoms too.

I wonder if you like the mountains as well as you do the sea. I am afraid I do, and better, even. It seems half disloyal to say so, for I was born here; to me there is rest and strength, and aspiration and exultation, among the mountains. They are nearly a day's journey from us — the White Mountains — but I will go, and get a glimpse and a breath of their glory, once a year, always. I was at Winnipiseogee, a mountain-girdled lake, in New Hampshire, when I saw your handwriting, first,—in a letter which told of your having been in Switzerland. We have no sky-cleaving Alps,—there is a massiveness, a breadth, about the hill scenery here, quite unlike them, I fancy. But such cascades, such streams as rise in the hard granite, pure as liquid diamonds, and with a clear little thread of music!

I usually stop at a village on the banks of the Pemigewasset, a small silvery river that flows from the Notch Mountains,—a noble pile, that hangs like a dream, and flits like one too, in the cloudy air, as you follow the stream's winding up to the

Flume, which is a strange grotto, cut sharply down hundreds of feet through a mountain's heart; an immense boulder was lodged in the cleft when it was riven, half way down, and there it forever hangs, over the singing stream. The sundered rocks are dark with pines, and I never saw anything lovelier than the green light with which the grotto is flooded by the afternoon sun. But I must not go on about the mountains, or I shall never stop, — I want to say something about our poets, but I will not do that, either.

Beauty drifts to us from the mother-land, across the sea, in argosies of poetry. How rich we are with Old England's wealth! Our own lies yet somewhat in the ore, but I think we have the genuine metal.

How true it is, as you say, that we can never utter the best that is in us, poets or not. And the great true voices are so, not so much because they can speak for themselves, but because they are the voices of our common humanity.

The poets are but leaders in the chorus of souls, — they utter our pæans and our *misereres*, and so we feel that they belong to us. It is indeed a divine gift, the power of drawing hearts upward through the magic of a song; and the anointed ones must receive their chrism with a holy humility. They receive but to give again, — "more blessed" so. And they may also receive the gratitude of those they bless, to give it back to God.

I hope you will write to me again some time,

though I am afraid I ought not to expect it. I know what it is to have the day too short for the occupations which *must* fill it, — to say nothing of what *might*, very pleasantly, too.

But I shall always be sincerely and gratefully yours, LUCY LARCOM.

TO J. G. WHITTIER.

BEVERLY, February 28, 1868.

MY DEAR FRIEND, — Nothing would be pleasanter to me than a visit to Amesbury, and the cold weather is no especial drawback. But I cannot be away from Beverly now, my mother is so ill. She has been suffering very much all winter, but is now nearly helpless, and I think she is rapidly failing. She has an experienced nurse with her, and there is little that any of us can do for her, except to look in now and then, and let her know that her children are not far away. That seems to be her principal earthly comfort. The coming rest is very welcome to her. She lies peacefully hoping for it, and she has suffered, and still does, such intense pain, I cannot feel as I otherwise would about her leaving us. But the rending of these familiar ties is always very hard to bear. She has been a good, kind mother to me, and it is saddest of all to see her suffer without the power of relief; to know that death only can end her pain.

I think of you often, and wish I could sit down for an evening by the light of your cheery wood fire, and have one of the old-time chats. I am so glad that A—— is there, to make it homelike. I think my most delightful remembrances of Amesbury are of that fireside, and the faces gathered about it, upon which the soft flow of the flames flickered and kindled, with the playful and varying interchange of thought. Last Sunday night I spent at Harriet Pitman's. Cold enough it was, too. But the greenhouse is a small edition of the tropics, and full of blossoms and sweet odors. I should want to live in it, if I were there.

I do not know what to make of the aspect of things at Washington. It cannot be that we shall be left to plunge into another war, and yet we may need it. I do not see that our terrible struggle made the deep impression it should in establishing national principles. Only apathy to the most vital interests could have brought us to this pass. It seems as if A. J. must show himself an absolute fiend, before his removal is insisted upon.

Miss Larcom's mother died March 14, 1868. The bereavement was great; but the long illness had prepared her daughter for the affliction. Years afterwards she used to say that when in trouble or despondency, like a child she wanted to cry out for her mother.

CHAPTER VIII.

WRITINGS AND LETTERS.

1868–1880.

THOUGH Miss Larcom's formal connection with school life ended when she left Norton, she continued to deliver occasional, and sometimes weekly, lectures at different schools, on topics illustrating English literature. In 1867, and at intervals for years after, at the Ipswich Academy, at Wheaton, at Dr. Gannett's school, and at Bradford Academy, the students never forgot her addresses on "Criticism," "Elizabethan Poetry," "The Drama," and "Sidney's 'Arcadia.'"

In spite of the fact that she received a fair salary from "Our Young Folks," and added to her resources by teaching and by printing poems in the magazines, it was necessary for her to practice economy. With the intention of being careful in her expenditures, she took rooms in Boston, purchasing and cooking her own food. She alluded to the plan thus: "In my housekeeping plan, I am going to carry out a pet notion. People generally prefer indigestible food, I find; at least, I cannot often get what I can digest. So I am going to teach myself to make unleavened bread, and all sorts of coarse-grained eatables, and these, with figs and dates, and baked apples, and a little meat now and then, will keep me in clover." Her friends, hearing of the way in which she "caricatured housekeeping," sent her boxes full of good things. It was with the pleasure of a school girl receiving a Thanksgiving box, that she acknowledged the receipt of eggs, cranberries, apples, and "such exquisitely sweet butter." She proved that with very little expense one can be happy, if the spirit is cheerful. This incident is an illustration of a lifetime of economical living.

The year 1868 was an important one to her, for in it her first volume of verse was printed. Influenced by the wishes of her friends for a keepsake, and feeling that, if she published, it would be a record of work done, and from it, as a mile-stone, she would be encouraged to do better verse-making in the future, she launched upon the literary market her book, entitled simply "Poems." It contained many of the lyrics upon which her fame as a poet will always be based. "Hannah," and "Skipper Ben," and "Hilary" have a place in it. "Hand in Hand with Angels" keeps before one the thought of unseen spiritual presences. "A Year in Heaven" reminds one of the life beyond, while "At the Beautiful Gate" expresses the longing of the soul for greater truth: —

> "Lord, open the door, for I falter,
> I faint in this stifled air."

The sweet quietude of "The Chamber called

Peace" surrounds the reader, for it merited Mr. Whittier's remark that "it is really one of the sweetest poems of Christian consolation I have read." The rich, full notes of "A Thanksgiving" are heard, as a human soul pours forth its earnest gratitude: —

"For the world's exhaustless beauty,
I thank thee, O my God!"

About this poem, Rev. J. W. Chadwick said to her, "Your "Thanksgiving" has become ritual in my church. If the people did not hear it every year, they would think the times were out of joint."

Miss Ingelow wrote her that she liked best "A White Sunday," with its hopeful lines, expressing "the earnest expectation of the creature:" —

"The World we live in wholly is redeemed;
Not man alone, but all that man holds dear:
His orchards and his maize; forget-me-not
And heart's-ease, in his garden; and the wild
Aerial blossoms of the untrained wood,
That makes its savagery so home-like; all
Have felt Christ's sweet Love watering their roots
His Sacrifice has won both Earth and Heaven."

The "Poems" were well received everywhere, and the reviewers were generally most complimentary. It was seen at once that a real poet, of true inspiration, had taken a permanent place in American literature. The musical modulations of the verse, with its tender lyrical quality, its local New England coloring, and its strong moral sentiment, soon gained her the affections of the people,

The name "Lucy Larcom" was now well known;

but, curiously enough, it was not associated with her personality, for it was thought to be a fictitious name, with "Apt alliteration's artful aid." A habit common among certain authors of the day was to have such euphonious *noms de plume* as "Minnie Myrtle," "Fanny Forrester," "Grace Greenwood;" and it was natural that "Lucy Larcom" should be classed with them. She often had amusing encounters with strangers about her identity. On the cars one day, a woman changed her seat for one in front of Miss Larcom, and, turning round, put the question, "Are you really Lucy Larcom, the poet? Some one said you were."

"Yes, that is my name."

"Then it is not a made-up name? Well, we never thought it was real when we read your pieces; and we thought you were younger."

"I am sorry to disappoint you."

"Oh! You don't disappoint me! I like the looks of you; only, people will have their ideas about poets."

A gentleman who had just been introduced to her was discussing the subject of names. He asked the derivation of her name; she told him that it was originally "Lark-Holme," the home of the larks; then he said, "Is there not some one who takes your name, and writes poetry, calling herself 'Lucy Larcom'? I never read any of the stuff."

In 1872, she did her first work of collaboration with Mr. Whittier. Conceiving the plan of printing a volume of poems dealing with the life of children, he secured her aid, and "Child-Life" was the first book which they produced in this way. He deferred to her judgment in the selection of the material, and, when doubtful, he always accepted her opinion. In sending her some poems for the collection, he wrote, "I leave thee to thy judgment; I think they will do, but I defer to thy wisdom." Her name is thus associated with the happy hours of many children, who were, and are, brought up on the wholesome verses of this nursery book. "The Owl and the Pussycat," "The Spider and the Fly," and "Philip, my King," with appropriate pictures, first became known to thousands of children, from this green-covered daily companion.

"Child-Life in Prose" came as a natural sequel to child-life in poetry; and Hawthorne's "Little Annie's Ramble," Lamb's "Dream Children," "The Ugly Duckling" of Hans Andersen, and "The Story without End," were made familiar through the medium of its pages.

Doubtless influenced by these publications, Miss Larcom decided to print, in a volume of her own, the children's poems she had written, especially those for "Our Young Folks;" so in 1873 her "Childhood Songs" appeared.

AMESBURY, November 25, 1874.

DEAR FRIEND, — I have just been looking over the beautiful book of "Childhood Songs," and my judgment is, that it is the best book of the kind I have ever seen. It has many poems, which, beside their adaptation to children, have a merit as lyrics, which I do not know where to look for in other collections of this sort. The heart is generally right in such books, but here head and heart are both satisfactory.

We did not get up so good a book as this in our "Child-Life." Thy friend,

J. G. Whittier.

TO MRS. MARY MAPES DODGE.

Beverly Farms, December 3, 1874.

Dear Mrs. Dodge, — The publishers assure me that they sent you a copy of "Childhood's Songs," as I requested. I hope you received it, at last. I care to have you like it, as a lover of children, quite as much as to have it spoken of in the magazine.

Your own little book must be nice; I hope to see it when I go to Boston.

Doubtless you are right about the verses. I always accept an editor's decision, without objecting, as I know the difficulties of the position. I will write when I can. For a month or two, I shall be specially busy, and possibly may not have time for "St. Nicholas," for which it is a pleasure to write.

Yours most truly, Lucy Larcom.

TO THE SAME.

Beverly Farms, December 30, 1874.

My dear Mrs. Dodge, — Your charming "Rhymes and Jingles" followed your pleasant note, and I thank you for both. The book is just what children most enjoy, as a real mother's book will be sure to be; and you have some sweet little poems which seem to hide themselves too modestly among the merry rhymes.

I think I have the mother-feeling, — ideally, at least; a woman is not a woman quite, who lacks it, be she married or single. The children — God bless them! — belong to the mother-heart that beats in all true women. They seem even dearer, sometimes, because I have none of my own to love and be loved by, for there is a great emptiness that only child-love can fill. So God made us, and I thank Him for it. The world's unmothered ones would be worse off if it were not so.

Thank you for writing of yourself, and your boys. I wish I knew you, face to face. I am sure we should find ourselves in sympathy in many ways.

I send a verse or two, for by and by, when the March winds blow.

When I get to a little clearing of leisure, I will write more for "St. Nicholas."

Truly your friend,

LUCY LARCOM.

TO MRS. J. T. FIELDS.

BEVERLY FARMS, December 5, 1875.

DEAR ANNIE, — I had a pleasant little visit at Mrs. Pitman's after I left you. We went to Professor Thayer's, in Cambridge, that evening, and heard Emerson's noble paper on "Immortality," which is soon to be published. There is great satisfaction in hearing such words from such a man's own lips, for we know that Emerson has as little as mortal can have of the haze of vanity between himself and the truth; and it is this surely, oftener than anything else, that blinds men's minds to the open secret of eternal life.

Mr. Longfellow was there, and I had a pleasant talk with him. He spoke of the book he is preparing and told me he wanted to put into it "Hannah Binding Shoes."

Mr. Garrison and Henry Vincent, the lecturer, were at Mrs. P.'s the next day.

I have been in Newburyport since I left Somerville, at my friend Mrs. Spalding's. Mr. Whittier came there on his way from Boston, and I did not see that he was the worse for the woman-avalanche that descended upon him at your door. . . .

In 1875, "An Idyl of Work," dedicated to working women, was issued by Osgood & Co. It is a long poem in blank verse, written chiefly in pentameters, and describes most beautifully the life of the Lowell factory girls, in "The Forties." There is a song of delight in work, running through it all. The incidents of prosaic labor are invested with a charm; and the toiler's lot is shown to have its bright side in the community of womanly interests that develop strong traits of character, and lead to lifelong attachments. It is an epic of labor, giving a history of an episode in American manufacture, that proved how mental and moral culture can be aided by hand-work, when the laborer looks upon his occupation as his privilege.

In the following year, "Roadside Poems," a well-edited compilation of mountain poetry, added a new interest to the country and the mountains, for the summer traveler. Shelley, Wordsworth, Longfellow, Browning, and Lowell, were made to act as interpreters of the wonders of the lane, and the beauty of the sunrise over mountain sanctuaries, and to explain the meaning of the storm reverberating among the hills. It is a little book filled with glimpses of the sky, the fragrance of flowers, the earth-smell of ferns, and the coloring of autumn leaves.

TO J. G. WHITTIER.

83 WALTHAM STREET, BOSTON,
January 1, 1878.

. . . Of course you must have grown very tired of the poetry written to you, and about you. I sent my verses to the "Transcript," because I thought you seemed too much pleased to think I had spared you the infliction! Discipline can never come too late in life, I am confident!

Still, I did n't say a word more than the truth, and I think I spoke sincerely for many others. It is a great thing to have won a nation's affection, — much greater than the greatest amount of mere fame.

Judging from our own inside view, none of us

deserve to be as well thought of by our friends as we are; but the beauty of it is, that real friendship knows us best after all, because it sees in us our best aim, endeavor, and possibilities, and lets our failures and imperfections pass by and be forgotten. Why not, when the judge is always so imperfect, too?

The sum of which is, that we all think you a pretty good sort of man, as men go.

Always thy friend,

LUCY LARCOM.

TO MRS. S. I. SPALDING.

83 WALTHAM STREET, January 17, 1878.

I have been reading the Book of Romans through, trying to forget that I had ever read it before, and I find that "justification by faith" seems to me a very different doctrine from the one I was brought up on. I don't know that I should understand it as Luther did. But it seems to me grander than I have dreamed of before. It is freedom to stand with our faces to the light, whatever our past may have been; freedom to do right from the love of it, and not as burdensome duty; and the love of doing right as the proof of deliverance. Is not this the "grace wherein ye stand," which Paul preached as free grace in Christ?

I find very little in the Book of Romans which points to some *future* salvation. It is the life redeemed from love of sin, which he seems to be talking to the Romans about. I do wish religion were made more practical in theology, after this Pauline fashion. I do not care for any commentator's judgment. I think that common sense and a sincere desire for truth will be shown the right interpretation. . . .

During part of the winter of 1878, Miss Larcom made her only foreign trip — a visit to Europe never being possible, on account of the expense — to Bermuda, which she thoroughly enjoyed. She wrote letters to the Boston "Daily Advertiser," describing the "Still vexed Bermoothes," with enthusiastic appreciation. The recollection of Miranda and Prospero, with "hag-born" Caliban, interested her as much as the houses with walls of coral, or the transparency of the beryl sea, through which one could see the sponges, and large purple amenones, and fish of brilliant hues. "A banana plantation is rather a shabby-looking affair; the leaves are beaten to tatters by the island tempests; but for a contrast there is the royal palm, to see which for the first time is an era in one's life, lifting its stately column above the cocoanut and India rubber trees. And we are satisfied that roses smell no less sweet for growing on the border of an onion patch. After all this wonder of foreign growths it is pleasant to see a dandelion in flower, and to find little mats of pimpernel on the hillside before our hotel. These little home-blossoms deepen the home feeling, and we are no more foreigners, even here."

A poem full of semi-tropical scenery, written on this trip, appeared in "Harper's Magazine:"—

"Under the eaves of a southern sky,
  Where the cloud-roof bends to the ocean floor,
Hid in lonely seas, the Bermoothes lie,
  An emerald cluster that Neptune bore
Away from the covetous earth-god's sight,
And placed in a setting of sapphire light."

For "pot-boilers," Miss Larcom undertook various inferior kinds of literary work, such as compilations of poetical calendars, and short biographical notices of famous people. One of her books of this class, "Landscape in American Poetry," with beautiful illustrations by Mr. J. Appleton Brown, was published in 1879. There was some original writing in it, but in the main, it was a collection from many sources, of poems dealing with interesting places in America.

TO MRS. E. B. WHEATON.

627 Tremont Street, Boston,
January 27, 1879.

My dear Mrs. Wheaton, — I have been intending to write, ever since I was at Norton, and tell you how much I enjoyed being there, and returning to the spirit of my old days at the Seminary.

I was so ill the last years of my stay there, I hardly knew how much of a home it was to me. To go back in restored health was a revelation of the old joy in my work. I think there must be something of the same feeling in looking back from the better world we hope for, when we have passed from this. We shall never know how good and beautiful a world we have lived in until we get away from it, and can get a glimpse of it with all our weariness and cares laid aside.

I think a great deal of the beautiful atmosphere which pervades the Norton life is due to the generous idea in which the school was founded. It gives the place a home feeling rarely found in such schools. Ever truly yours,

LUCY LARCOM.

TO MRS. S. I. SPALDING.

BOSTON, December 6, 1879.

When I came home from the reception and breakfast given to Dr. Holmes on Wednesday, I thought I would sit down and write you about it at once. . . . The breakfast was a splendid success; you have probably read about it, but there was a certain exhilaration in being in the presence of so many bright people, and feeling perfectly at home, which was indescribable. I never expected to enjoy anything of the kind at all, but I was really taken off my feet, in a figurative sense. Dr. Holmes filled the place of honor in a delightful manner. It was really like sitting down at his own breakfast table. Mrs. Whitney and I went at twelve as invited. I left at a little past six and they were not through with their letters and speeches then. I was introduced to ever so many people I never saw before.

. . . I don't know but the pleasantest thing to me was the opportunity of speaking to Rev. Phillips Brooks, or rather of hearing him speak face to face. To look up into his honest, clear eyes, was like seeing the steady lights in a watch-tower; and a tower of strength he is among us. The outward largeness of the man is a type of his moral strength and mental breadth and spiritual height, I am more than ever convinced. I never spoke to a man who seemed so thoroughly grand to me.

Mr. Whittier came, but remained a very short time. I saw him only a moment, just before we went in. My escort — they were all coupled off by a printed plan — was Mr. William Winter, a New York poet and journalist. He was very entertaining, and I think his poem was the best and most effective of the occasion.

. . . I am fast getting to be a dissipated woman, but I must and will put myself to work steadily for a week or two.

This was the first meeting between Miss Larcom and Mr. Brooks. She had heard him preach at Trinity Church and was greatly helped by his sermons, for which she had often thanked him by letter, and, in return, had received some few characteristic lines, like the following: —

BOSTON, April 14, 1879.

MY DEAR MISS LARCOM, — The preaching of Christ as a personal friend and Saviour of all our souls becomes to me more and more the one interesting work of life, and the readiness of the people to hear that one simple message, which, in its endlessly various forms, is always the same, gives me ever new satisfaction and delight.

I have known you by your verses for years. I hope some day we may meet.

Yours very truly,

PHILLIPS BROOKS.

The friendship between them deepened, as the years went on. They had many serious conversations on spiritual subjects, and he became to her the great religious guide of her life. His personality, with its earnest, and even fierce, love for the simplicity of truth, and the power with which he presented it, made the deepest impression upon her in her last decade, and brought to the fruition of spiritual loveliness the remaining years of her career.

BOSTON, March 20, 1880.

MY DEAR MISS LARCOM, — You will allow me to thank you for your note and to say how truly glad I am if anything I said on Wednesday evening helped you in your thought of the Lord's Supper. To me the Personalness of the great Sacrament seems to be the key to all its meaning, and its simplicity is its grandeur and its charm.

Ever yours sincerely,

PHILLIPS BROOKS.

TO MRS. S. I. SPALDING.

627 TREMONT STREET,
February 12, 1880.

. . . You must be disheartened often, in having to listen to the vagaries of the many who have ordained themselves prime ministers of divine affairs. I really cannot feel it right to put myself in the way of hearing such talk.

What can the end be, since there is common sense among the people, but a disgust for preaching altogether?

But I believe in a movement towards a service in which worship shall be the chief element; and I don't think I am a step nearer Episcopacy, either. I am trying to like that, because I have always been unjustly prejudiced against it, but I am a born Independent at heart. . . .

The years of Miss Larcom's greatest poetical production were brought to a close by the printing, in 1880, of "The Wild Roses of Cape Ann." Her works were bound together in a Household Edition, in 1884. After this, she wrote continually for the magazines, and on anniversary occasions of various kinds. Some of these verses were included, with a few new ones, in the booklet "Easter Gleams," and in the selection of religious poems, called "At the Beautiful Gate," but no noted additions were made to her poems after this, though there are many of her lines of great beauty, scattered through the pages of current ephemeral literature, up to the time of her death.

TO S. T. PICKARD.

BETHEL, ME., September 30, 1880.

MY DEAR MR. PICKARD, — I go to-morrow to Berlin Falls, New Hampshire, to stay at the Cascade House until I have finished reading my proof.[1] I wish to thank you for your interest in the book about to be. It will have more character and more local color than the other; but I do not write for critics, but for my friends, as the dedication will show, and I do not care much whether critics like it or not, provided my friends do.

I can conceive of no greater damper upon one's poetic attempts than the cold water of criticism. It is from heart to heart, from friend to friend, that I write; and I find in that the highest inspiration to do my best. Of course I am glad to enlarge the circle of my friends in this way; and poetry has amply repaid me in the coin of friendship. One gives out life in writing; and nothing but life in return — life enlarged and filled — gives any true satisfaction. Of course I shall send you a copy, not editorially, but personally.

The "Wild Roses" were fragrant, and delighted some of the critics, even, for in addition to those that grew along Cape Ann, there were many culti-

[1] *Wild Roses of Cape Ann.*

vated ones, that blossomed beside the still waters of thought, and in the quiet retreats of meditation: —

> "A Rose is sweet,
> No matter where it grows: and roses grow
> Nursed by the pure heavens, and the strengthening earth,
> Wherever men will let them. Every waste
> And solitary place is glad for them,
> Since the old prophets sang, so, until now."

"Phebe" has a prominent place in the book — the poem that drew from Mr. Howells, when he was editor of the "Atlantic," a most graceful note of acceptance: —

My dear Miss Larcom, — You take rejections so sweetly, that I have scarcely the heart to accept anything of yours. But I do like "Phebe," and I am going to keep her.

"Shared" excited admiration; and was pronounced by one competent critic to be the best religious lyric of the decade: —

> "The air we breathe, the sky, the breeze,
> The light without us and within,
> Life, with its unlocked treasuries,
> God's riches, are for all to win."

The theological poem, "The Heart of God," was the cause of controversy. A stranger wrote, asking her to change it, for he thought it expressed too clearly "the old doctrine of the Divinity of Christ." She answered politely, but with a strong statement of her faith, that what he called "the old Doctrine" was the inspiration of the verses: "To me, Christ is the Infinite Person, at once human and divine. God exists as impersonal Spirit, but I know Him only as a person through Christ. The historical Christ is entirely true to me, as the only way in which God could humanly be known to us. It is no more impossible for me to believe that the "Eternal Christ of God," the personal manifestation of Deity, should veil Himself for a time with the human form, than that we, in our humble personality, as sharers of the Divine Nature, should wear it as we do." The same truth she put strongly in "Our Christ," when she wrote: —

"In Christ I feel the Heart of God."

Concerning this poem, the Rev. W. Garrett Horder, the English hymnologist, writes that it has been accorded a place in "Hymns Supplemental" for Congregational churches, and was sung for the first time in England, February 14, 1894, in Colby Chapel, Bradford.

In making an analytical study of Miss Larcom's poetry, the range of her verse becomes apparent. She finds expression for her muse in almost all forms of versification: the epic, as in "An Idyl of Work;" the ballad, with its merry lines, relating some story of early New England days, or some delightful old legend; the lyric in its numerous forms, — pastoral songs that breathe of the fields and pretty farms, lyrics of nature in her peaceful moods when the wayside flower dwells securely, or in her grander moods when the mountains hide themselves in storm-clouds, or the sea moans in the deepening tempest; lyrics of grief, when, in solemn and plaintive strains, she chants the dirge of Elizabeth Whittier, or tolls the passing bell of Lincoln, or sheds a tear over the grave of Garfield; and sacred lyrics, in which she deals with the deepest emotions of the human heart, expressing its longing after immortality, and its adoration for God. The range of her verse is further enlarged by the addition of the sonnet's "narrow plot of ground," and the stately movement of the ode.

Her lines always have a musical flow born of intense emotion. They have a smoothness and ripple, like the flow of the summer brook, or the even modulations of the tides. At times, they possess a cadence not unlike what Mr. Arnold, speaking of Spenser, calls "fluidity,"—an effect produced by combinations of melodious sounds, as in these lines from "On the Beach:"—

> "And glimmering beach, and plover's flight,
> And that long surge that rolls
> Through bands of green and purple light,
> Are fairer to our human sight
> Because of human souls."

Again, in "Golden-Rod:"—

> "The swinging harebell faintly tolled
> Upon the still autumnal air,
> The golden-rod bent down to hold
> Her rows of funeral torches there."

And in "My Mountain:" —

> "I shut my eyes in the snow-fall,
> And dream a dream of the hills;
> The sweep of a host of mountains,
> The flash of a hundred rills."

Together with the music, there is strength in her verses, when she attempts to deal with subjects that call for vigorous treatment. In the "Rose Enthroned," there is a strong grasping at the origin of things, and powerful descriptions of the primeval birth-throes that, from the war of elements, issued forth in the fairness of creation.

> "Built by the warring elements they rise,
> The massive earth-foundations, tier on tier,
> Where slimy monsters with unhuman eyes
> Their hideous heads uprear."

In her mountain descriptions there is the same power. The wind-beaten and thunder-scarred summit of Whiteface presents itself to her as the visage of a monarch, who seems to rule the race of giant hills. The effect of a mountain whose slopes plunge into the sea is graphically given in the phrase, "Plunged knee-deep in yon glistening sea." Her appreciation for beautiful details of nature, that seemed to escape the common observer, is seen in her similes and epithets; the little streams winding through the marshes are called "sea-fed creeks;" the mists that rise in the evening, reflecting the light of the descending sun, are "violet mists;" the quiet of the fields of clover, when one is out of sound of the waves, are fitly called "sweet inland silences;" the heart of the woods, where are the shadows, has its "forest crypts;" and there are "mosaics of tinted moss."

Dr. Holmes very well describes her when he says: "She was as true a product of our Essex County soil as the bayberry; and her nature had the chaste and sweet fragrance of its fair and wholesome leaves. She was a true poetess, and a noble woman." Her writings have the genuine flavor of the soil, like the perfume of the woods, or the salt spray that bathes one's face along the seashore. Mr. Whittier thus analyzed her powers as a poet: "She holds in rare combination the healthfulness of simple truth and common sense, with the fine and delicate fancy, and an artist's perception of all beauty." Mr. Stedman, in his "Poets of America," speaks of her as a sweet-voiced singer of "orchard notes." This is a good partial description of certain of her songs, but as an estimate of her poetical ability it is very limited. She was not disturbed by the criticism, but wrote thus to a friend.

TO MRS. S. I. SPALDING.

4 Hotel Byron, Berkeley Street,
Boston, March 8, 1886.

. . . Don't be troubled about "orchard-notes." I consider it the highest compliment.

Think of goldfinches and linnets, song-sparrows and orioles! I know and love their separate songs, and should feel proud if I thought *my* singing deserved comparison with theirs. Why, three fourths of the cheer of the spring and summer-time is in those same orchard-notes! I shall have to try hard to live up to my reputation. But if you do think I get up a little higher into the air, a little farther off into the wilderness sometimes, for a more meditative flight of song, just remember that very high critics do not always comprehend the music in the air about them. Does not Milton write of Shakespeare as "Fancy's child," and of his poetry as "wood-notes wild"?

Such an estimate must be imperfect, because it leaves out of consideration the moral power of her religious writings, which, more than her nature-songs, have won for her a place in the regard of the people. A gentleman thanking her for the gift of one of her books, expressed for many readers a recognition of this deeper hold: "A soul once fed and inspired as was mine, at a critical and sad juncture of its life, by your poetry, is likely to open, as I did, the beautiful book your kindness sent me, with strange delight." One who could write "A Thanksgiving," with its noble lines, —

> "For thine own great gift of Being,
> I thank Thee, O my God,"

and the words, —

> "Lord, enter this house of my being
> And fill every room with Thy light," —

should certainly be called a religious poet of a high order; and her poems are filled with such passages as that which follows, presenting religious thought simply and convincingly: —

> "God hears
> The prayer the good man means, the Soul's desire,
> Under whatever rubbish of vain speech;
> And prayer is, must be, each man's deepest words.
> He who denies its power, still uses it,
> Whenever he names God, or thinks of Him."

Poetry, to her, was vastly more than word-shaping, or combinations of accented and unaccented syllables; it was an attitude of mind and soul towards all existence, a view-point of her being, from which she saw such visions, and heard such sounds, that the impulse was irresistible to record in recognized poetic form her ideas and feelings. She found poetry in everything around her; it was the atmosphere she breathed, the medium, like imponderable ether, through which she saw life. Nature had a more profound meaning to her than the charm of color, or the changing pleasures of the land or the sea. It was the visible evidence of the unseen, the prophecy of a greater fulfillment, the proclamation of the spiritual element within, which the senses of themselves could not perceive. She once said, "Nature is one vast metaphor through which spiritual truth may be read:" —

> "The Universe is one great loving Thought,
> Written in Hieroglyphs of bud and bloom."

The delicate and spiritual nature of womanhood, too, with its heroism, breathed through all she wrote. Everything she touched glowed with the light of purity. Her aim was to uplift and sweeten life, by a revelation of its true meaning. Her measures are choice; her passion is genuine; her verses sincere; and the *morale* of them is always elevating.

Our literature is not rich in women poets of the highest genius, but there are many who have sung true songs. Maria Lowell was permitted to give us a few notes only of her chaste singing. The Cary sisters, Mrs. Cook, Mrs. Greenough, and Helen Hunt Jackson, and many who now enliven our magazines, have done genuine work; but one often looks in vain for the power that distinguished Miss Larcom. Considering the range of the versification, the music of the lines, the strength of phrase and beauty of metaphor, and lofty moral intensity of her poetry, it is not claiming too much to say that it exhibits a genius as versatile and as rich in its utterance as that of any of her female contemporaries, and considering the impression that she has made upon the people, at their firesides and in their worship, she holds a place, equal to any, in their hearts.

Her poems have been recognized in many collections in our land and in England. Mr. Longfellow in his "Poems of Places" has remembered her. She is honored in Emerson's "Parnassus;" one of her hymns is included in Dr. Martineau's "Hymns of the Spirit;" she has been given a place, by Mr. Garrett Horder, in "A Treasury of Sacred

Song from American Sources;" by Mr. Higginson, in "American Sonnets;" by Mr. Richard Grant White, in "The Poetry of the Rebellion;" and by Mr. W. M. Rossetti, in his "English Selections from Popular Poets."

The following letter to Dr. John Hunter of Glasgow shows that she enjoyed this recognition of her work: —

BEVERLY, MASS., July 10, 1890.

DEAR SIR, — A friend gave me your "Hymns of Faith and Life," in the winter, telling me she had found one or two of mine in it. On looking it over, I find five, not all of which are credited to me, though all are included in the Household Edition of my poems, published by Houghton, Mifflin & Co. I thought you would like to know the authorship, and therefore write.

Of course I am gratified to know that my hymns were taken on their own merit apparently, and I am glad if anything I have written is a natural expression of sincere worship for other hearts and voices than my own. Truly yours,

LUCY LARCOM.

The two following letters illustrate how Dr. Holmes and Mr. Longfellow appreciated Miss Larcom's work.

296 BEACON STREET, November 17, 1880.

MY DEAR MISS LARCOM, — I have been reading your poems at all the spare moments I could find this evening. Many of them I read carefully — every page I tasted. My wife and daughter were sitting opposite to me, and I had to shade my eyes with my hand that they should not see the tears shining in them — this over and over again. The poems are eminently wholesome, sweet, natural. Their perfume is as characteristic of the soil they spring from as that of the sweet fern or the bayberry.

It is pleasant to me to find my name in such good company as it is in your pages, and if anything I have written has ever given you pleasure this volume has amply repaid me.

Very sincerely yours,

O. W. HOLMES.

P. S. (Worth all the rest). I got a letter from Mr. Whittier which reads as follows: —

"Has thee seen Miss Larcom's "Cape Ann"? I like it, and in reading it I thought thee would also. Get it and see if she has not a right to stand with the rest of us. Wishing thee a pleasant Thanksgiving after the manner of the enclosed card, I am faithfully thy friend, J. G. WHITTIER."

CAMBRIDGE, December 24, 1880.

DEAR MISS LARCOM, — I thank you very much for your beautiful volume of beautiful poems. I have been reading it this morning with great enjoyment.

I always liked your poetry, and now like it more

than ever. It is not merely verse, but possesses the true poetic instinct and insight.

One little song among the many particularly charms me. It is "At her Bedside." It ought to be set to music. Thanks, and all good wishes.

Sincerely yours,

HENRY W. LONGFELLOW.

CHAPTER IX.

RELIGIOUS CHANGES.

1881–1884.

The true poetic temperament has in it an element of religion; for religion and poetry both deal with the spiritual interpretation of life, and one who possesses the temperament for either is conscious of the vastness overshadowing common things, and sees the infinite meaning of the apparent finiteness of the visible world. The delicate perception of truth which is a distinctive quality of the poet often leads to the deep appreciation of the spirit in and through nature, and enables one to feel and know God.

Lucy Larcom possessed the poetic temperament, with this strong element of religion. She was preeminently religious, in the sense of possessing a spiritual power, dealing continually with spiritual things. She began early to interpret life in the light of divine truth; and truth made real in human character she considered the one thing worth striving for.

Her relations to organized Christianity are particularly interesting. Doubtless the history of her connection with the churches is a type of that of other lives numerous in our generation that have become dissatisfied with the communions in which they have been trained, and after a period of uncertainty and unrest have found a home in the Episcopal Church.

Her religious life began in a Puritan home, and in a Congregational meeting-house. The strong ethical teaching of her fathers made a lasting impression on her, and the dogmatic preaching of Calvinism influenced her young life. From both she gained a love for the simplicity of living which characterized her career, and that clearness of conscience which she always displayed. There was also a joy to her under the austerity of the worship, and the sternness of the theology. The sermons suggested new thoughts, which forced themselves between the sentences of the minister, and in this way she preached to herself another sermon than that spoken from the pulpit.

Her religious enthusiasm bore fruit at thirteen years of age, in church membership, in Lowell. Not many years after this she was sorry for the step she had taken, for the natural broadening of her mind and the deepening of her consciousness of truth led her far away from the doctrines she had accepted. The sermons that she heard did not seem to satisfy her needs; she longed for spiritual nourishment, for help on the daily path, for thoughts that had some connection with actual temptations and doubts. Most of the discourses dealt ingeniously with exegetical questions, or were massive arguments used to crush the objector, or efforts to prove some metaphysical doctrine. Relating one Sunday's experience, which has been referred to before in her diary, she said, "I went to meeting, expecting and needing spiritual food, and received only burning coals and ashes. There was a sermon to prove that Satan will be tormented for ever and ever; and the stress of the argument was to prove the endlessness of his punishment."

Not only did she find a failing sympathy with the preaching and worship, but there were doctrines she could not continue to hold. Among these doctrines were, verbal inspiration of the Bible, which she thought mechanical and destructive of the Spirit's influence through a distinctive human personality; the Atonement, as the purchase blood of God's favor for a fallen race; predestination, which seemed to eliminate man's freedom; and endless punishment, adjudged for acts in this life, without any probation in a future state, which seemed to her contrary to the idea of the Sonship of man. Neither did she care for the emphasis placed on doctrine, as distinguished from life. The central point in her theology was the truth of God's love, and from this, by logical sequence, came her ideas of His revelation through nature, through human life as His gift, and through character as a manifestation of His glory. She was a student of Maurice, who led her along congenial paths of thought. On Sundays when she remained away from church, she generally read a sermon of Robertson's; and in his powerful analyses of truth, and in his burning love for the Master, she found continued inspiration. Her love for the person of Jesus increased each year. She felt herself a member of the Invisible Church, being contented with the thought that the visible churches had no claim upon her, because of their errors.

TO J. G. WHITTIER.

627 Tremont Street,
Boston, December 25, 1881.

My dear Friend, — Alone in my room this evening, I feel just like writing a Christmas letter to you, and I follow the impulse.

This day always brings back old times and old friends to memory, but never with sadness to me, because the one idea of the day is hope and joy for all souls, the possibilities of infinite help, unending progress. Whenever I enter deeply into the thought of Christ, whenever I feel Him the one Reality inseparable from my own being, then I feel that I have my friends safe, and that they are to be my friends forever. To me, He is the one Divine Friend in whom human friendships can alone be real and permanent, because He draws us into sympathy with what is best, with what is eternal, the love of goodness, the consciousness of God in us and around us, and the solemn gladness of a human life into which God has entered, and where He still is.

God with us still, the Spiritual Presence of One

who is more real than any other person can be to us, through whom indeed we receive our personality, — this idea, so grand as at times to seem almost impossible, grows more definite and clear to me. It is the "So I am with you alway" of Christ. And with this idea, that of those whom we love unseen, our friends who have disappeared from sight, becomes more definite also.

Sometimes I can say undoubtingly, "I *know* I shall find them again, where He is." But though the light flickers and dims sometimes, what if it does? There the light is, and every year a larger space is redeemed from darkness.

Oh, my dear friend! life is a gift blessed as it is awful. To think how close we are to one another for good or evil, do what we will! We cannot be apart from our fellow-beings; the pulses of this life we have in common throb, upward or downward, through us forever. Death is not to me half so solemn as life: but then death is no reality — a circumstance of our external life only. . . .

TO THE SAME.

627 Tremont Street,
Boston, June 6, 1881.

. . . I am steadily gaining in strength I think, and I am glad to keep on learning to live and to work, with such limitations as years necessarily bring. I find my life taking deeper hold of all other human lives; I feel myself more closely and warmly one of the great human family, every year of my life. And I feel through this the assurance of immortality — because we are in our deepest instincts children of the living God — because we, as sons and daughters, are united through the Son with the Father; we share His eternity; we cannot lose Him nor one another, nor the least spark of truth or love kindled within us from His being.

I am glad that I live, and that I shall die; that I shall fall asleep to awake with all I love, with all that is permanent here, in Him.

The forward outlook is full of good cheer; for is not He the Eternally Good? . . .

TO FRANKLIN CARTER.

BEVERLY, MASS., July 18, 1881.

DEAR FRANK, — I want to write a word of congratulation to you, in your new position. C—— told me you thought of going to Williamstown, but I did not know it was fully decided, until I saw your address in a Boston paper.

It was an excellent inaugural. I felt my sympathy go out to you as I read. I felt sure, and feel sure, that you will do good in your new position, which surely is a most responsible one, in a time like this. I wonder if it is really a time of greater unbelief than hitherto. Doubt is not an unhealthy symptom; it argues the possibility of belief. Indifference to high truth seems to me worst of all, the indifference that comes of *too much world*, which everybody seems to get suffocated in.

It is a great privilege to be able to influence young men to the best things, as you will be able to, — to make low aims seem, as they are, unworthy of manhood. God bless you and help you!

I have lived on, doing the little I could, during these last few years. I have gained in health, and am always hoping to return to some steady work; but it may not be best to do so at all. I like my freedom, and if I can afford to keep it, I shall. I am sure it is not good for me to live in a school. I sometimes wish I had earned or inherited money enough not to have to think of the future, but doubtless the Lord knows just what I need. It is not best for us all to have life made easy for us, in that way.

As I look back on my life, I see much reason for humility. I ought to have done so much more and so much better. Nevertheless the future is bright, for God is good. Sometimes it seems to me as if I were just learning what His forgiveness means, what it is to begin every day anew, as if there had been no unworthy past, as if there were only His love and my desire to please Him left. But I only meant to write a line. I go from here to spend the "hay-fever" season among the mountains very soon.

Always and truly yours,

LUCY LARCOM.

The change in Miss Larcom's religious life came when she began to attend the services of Trinity Church, Boston, in 1879. The preaching of Phillips Brooks was the realization, in living words, of her own thought. He gave utterance for her to all her broader and freer conceptions of Christianity. She had known little of the Episcopal Church before going to Trinity, and she had the same inherited prejudices that many, bred like her, have, though she remembered with pleasure St. Ann's in Lowell, during her days of wage earning; but the simplicity of the worship at Trinity, and the earnestness of the preacher, touched the deepest chords in her life, and she realized that she could be helped by them. Writing to one of her friends, who urged upon her the claims of the Episcopal Church, she said: —

. . . I have been very much interested in the services at Trinity Church. Just think! two prayer-books came to me in one week! one from a friend in New York, from whom I had not heard for a year. I do not know what special suggestion I am to get from the fact, except that I am to know more of the Episcopal Church. Truly I am ashamed of my ignorance regarding it. I enjoy the services, but I think I still strongly prefer Congregational ways. If only there were a little more sharing of the worship on the part of the people! I don't like to think that the minister is doing it all up for me; but that is the way of one, and not of the other, decidedly. I am going to be able to worship with Episcopalians as intelligently as with others. . . .

At another time she wrote about her church connections as follows: —

. . . I wish I could feel as you do, about the Church. I should like to be there, but I have to look upon it from the outside as an institution. The real church, to which I hope I belong, seems to me to be so much broader than any one form, so inclusive of all denominations, that I hardly think I have the right to identify myself with any; for, by so doing, I should exclude myself absolutely from the rest. Now I seem to myself to belong everywhere. Yet it is sometimes lonely to feel that spiritually I have not where to lay my head. We women crave home, a home of our own; but we must not deceive ourselves by shutting our eyes, and making believe we are at home, when we are not.

However, I mean to go regularly to Trinity if I can, for the feeling of having free seats is more comfortable than that of intruding into people's pews, and I go as if I had a right to the service. . . .

Her diary for 1881 and 1882 indicates the deepening of her religious thought, and the way in which the Episcopal Church was becoming known to her.

Boston, November 28, 1881. Waked by distant bells of Advent Sunday. As a Puritan, I have known little of the Christian year, in its Church history. It is worth while to try to enter into the spirit of all methods of true Christian worship. I read a sermon by F. D. Maurice, one by F. W. Robertson, and one by Phillips Brooks, all bearing upon the idea of these Advent days. In the "Christian Year" (Keble), an allusion is made to one of the skeptical centuries, which seems to fit this, in its over-scientific tendencies: —

> "An age of light,
> Light without love, glares on the aching sight."

But under all true science, — if science is indeed knowledge, — we shall find Christ, since Christ is the revelation of the deepest love of God.

December 4. Have been writing Christmas verses, by request, the past week. Thanksgiving and Christmas would blend themselves in my thoughts as one festival. "For my body liveth by my soul, and my soul by me" (St. Augustine). "Too little doth he love Thee, who loves anything with thee, which he loveth not for Thee" (*Ibid.*).

December 5. Two distinct thoughts impressed by the two successive evening services at Trinity Church: —

A week since, — That the controversy between skepticism and Christianity, as carried on quite recently among us, does not touch the real point in question, which is whether Christ, the Son of God, has come into the world, and has changed it, and is changing it for the better: not whether certain statements of the Hebrew Scriptures can be verified as facts, but whether there is a living Christ.

And last evening, — That the motive of the Christian life, the true reason why we should become Christians, and live as Christians, is that other men may receive the blessing; that it may widen on, through us, into unknown ages. It was a carrying out of St. Paul's thought, spoken to the Ephesians, about the Gentile world and the "ages to come." It is the grandeur of Christianity that it will not permit us to shut ourselves up in our own personal or local interests, — that it belongs to the whole race, and unites us to every human heart.

A note from Mrs. Garfield this morning. Though so nearly a stranger, she lets me in, a little way, to the sacred seclusion of her sorrow, — "this valley and this shadow," as she calls it. She cannot see why the blow had to fall upon her, — nor can we see why the country needed it. The blasphemous conceit of the assassin, who claims to have been inspired by the Deity, makes it all the more perplexing.

One good thing ought to come of this trial, — that we should all of us try to know clearly what we mean, when we claim close relations with the Divine Being. Too many, perhaps all of us, sometimes, use His name insanely, and therefore irreverently, in our thoughts, and to cloak our errors to ourselves.

Begin this morning Max Müller's "Science of Religion," which I have never yet thoroughly read.

January 1, 1882. Heard the midnight toll of the passing Old Year at Trinity Church last night. It was good to be there, and to come out into the clear starlight and moonlight of the New Year, with the great company that had reverently gathered in the church to watch the coming in of 1882, — another Year of Our Lord. Rev. Mr. ——'s sermon was appropriate, but that old, sad, haunting thought seemed to me to be too painfully impressed, — that, whatever we do, the scars of our past sins eternally remain, — that the losses caused by our wrong-doing can never be made up. Is it the true reading of God's forgiveness in Christ? Is not the uplifting power of the new love with which His Spirit floods our life, something nobler than we should have known, except for the pain, and the wounding, and the loss that came of sin? For the evil that has come to others through us, may not a flood of good out of the heart of our loving Christ overflow all, and lift them, with us, to a higher stratum of life? — I must believe it — that righteousness in human souls will obliterate the past evil. If it is to be remembered no more, it must not *be* there, — or some better thing must have come in its place. We cannot tell how far God's love may extend, what miracles it works. The chapter about the New Jerusalem coming down from God out of heaven, was read as the year was passing, and Mr. Brooks made that the point of his remarks, — that the coming year might be the New Jerusalem to us. In that light all darkness may surely be forgotten.

January 6, Epiphany. Went to the Church service. The thought that Christ truly came to us, to all the world, through His birth at Bethlehem, and the joy of His coming, is a blessing that everybody may share, and that it is more truly a blessing because it is to be shared, was chiefly dwelt upon. It struck me as a new thought, that the Wise Men from the East represented all the science, all the intellectual treasure of all time, which are truly given to humanity only when laid at the feet of Christ. The preacher did not express that idea, but it passed through my mind as I listened. Every gift we have, every work we do, only becomes a real, living, worthy thing, when given to Christ to be inspired with His life. If the scientific research of this age could but see the star hanging over the place where the Young Child lies, and find its true illumination in Him!

January 7. Miss H—— called, full of enthusiasm over what she believes herself to have done by healing the sick, through the power of prayer. I must believe that what she says is true, — and yet I question. Can this be God's way? Not impossible — but I have never been able to see that any prayer for definite physical results was so good as that which asks to be brought into harmony with the will of God, so that we shall accept any condition which He sees best for us. Yet — what does the "gift of healing" mean — if not that He permits health to flow through one life into another? My little crippled friend, E——, does not feel sure that she ought to ask God to make her well and strong, like other girls. I wish she might be, though.

January 8. Miss E. H. called. Our talk always gets back to the one subject, — Christ in human life. She cannot see that He is more than the best of all human helpers, and yet she has flashes of higher truth sometimes. I think she wishes for a definite intellectual idea of the Christ, for she said to me, "You make it wholly spiritual," — and so the conception of him, in the human soul, must be, it seems to me. She said, "I think of what He was," and I think of Him, that He *is*, and there we parted.

It is to me like the sunlight: clear, penetrating, inspiring, the idea of Christ who is, was, and is to be, the Eternal Son of the Father, the presence of God in humanity, as the friend of every soul, — the uniting link between the human and the divine. I feel my own personal immortality in following this truth whithersoever it may lead, — deeper, ever deeper, into the Heart of God, as I earnestly believe.

At church the subject was the power behind all human efforts, which makes them worth anything. The planter and the waterer are nothing, except as means bringing the seed to growth, which must first be alive, a force in itself, which he who tends cannot produce or understand. The power of God behind all worthy human efforts, that we are tools in the Master's hand, and must refer every good result to Him, were the inferences.

Who can explain moods? A strange depression has been over me to-day, as of some impending danger to some life near to mine. I shook it off in going out, but I found myself imagining the saddest thing that could possibly happen to me or my friends, or the country, or the world. I do not think I dread any one thing for myself, yet the removal of some of my friends would leave life very lonely.

January 16. Yesterday I was much instructed and helped by reading one or two of Maurice's sermons. The thought that forgiveness means the putting away of sins is not often emphasized as he does it, — "Power *on earth* to forgive sins;" that here one can lay down the burden, and go on fighting the enemy with a sure hope of conquest, because of that divine life and strength that comes through a present Christ; — this is release indeed. Not that we shall be forgiven, but that we are forgiven, if we turn to the truth in the love of it.

And the thought of the Communion service as a marriage-supper, a token that our lives are reunited to the divine life, came to me with new force.

Mr. Brooks preached about heaven, in the afternoon; that it must be the continuance of life, — of the highest and deepest we know here. There always will be for us, God, and the "charity" which means love. He spoke from chapter xiii., I. Corinthians: "For now we see through a glass darkly," — carrying out the image of life blurred and distorted often to us here, made clear there, where only true things can remain. Keble says, for yesterday, that we may —

> "Through the world's sad day of strife
> Still chant his morning song."

And why should not the music of heaven be the continuing of what is the true harmony of earth? It must be. The sermon yesterday referred especially to the death of two ministers in the Church the past week, Dr. Stone and John Cotton Smith.

January 23. Remarks at table, where surely people talk very freely. One lady says that she has never for an hour been glad that she was born. I can scarcely think of such a thing as possible, because it is God's world, and if we have any real glimpse of Him we must know that there is a divine purpose in our being here, even if we do not have the "good time" in life that we think we deserve. But it may be an inherited morbid feeling, it may be an affectation, — it may be several things.

Another lady states her Unitarian position that "Christ was human, we know, — he must also have been more than human, else he could not help us, therefore he was divine; but he could not have been wholly divine, else he could not have been an example for us." The last assertion is to me untrue. He must be able to help us more, because He is one with the Father, nor is He less our example, but more. He never gave a lower standard than this, — "Be ye perfect, even as your Father in heaven is perfect." He surely made God our only example of goodness, to learn and to follow. And we know that we are made in the image of God, because we cannot in our best moments accept any standard but this, — of perfection to be sought after through eternity; the grandeur of our being is that there will always be something beyond for us to seek.

Reading "Ecce Homo" for the first time, with a view to studying the "Life of Christ" with a friend.

February 6. Reading Renan's "Life of Jesus." In the introduction, his objections to the fourth Gospel seem to me to arise from some lack of perception in himself. I cannot find in it the "pretentious, heavy, badly written tirades" to which he alludes. Nor does it seem to me anything against the book that it was written from memory, long after the death of Christ. To apply to so close a friendship as that between Jesus and John the passage, "Our memories are transformed with all the rest; the idea of a person whom we have known changes with us," seems to me a wholly unsatisfactory and unappreciative way of putting it. If friends, and such friends, do not remember each other as they really are, we lose the idea of personal identity altogether. Yet Renan seems to think that John did write the fourth Gospel, and from the same close kind of intimacy as that which existed between Socrates and Plato. We surely reach the heart of Christ most closely through the words of the beloved disciple, — the stories clustering around the birth of Christ, which Renan dismisses as "legendary," seem to be so simply on his assertion. Were they so, the character of Jesus, Son of God and Son of Man, remains itself divinely alone in the world's history. But I cannot see more miracle in the beginning than all the way through. Nor does it seem to me that it would have been more sacrilegious for Him to say "I am God," which he never did in words affirm, Renan says, than to say, as He did, "I and my Father are one;" "He that hath seen me hath seen the Father." He spoke as the Son of Man, referring also always to His Father, claiming to be, in the closest sense, the Son of God. As a man, He must refer to the God beyond Him, else He could not have made Himself understood by men. For myself, I cannot think of God at all, except as having eternally this human side, by which we human beings, His children, may know Him. There is no unity in the idea of Him without this complexity, which shows Him as Father, Son, and Spirit.

Yet Christ's human life was perfectly human, wholly so; and the picturesque beauty of that life, the lovely scenery of Nazareth, and his wayfaring company of disciples, plain countrymen, group themselves very attractively on Renan's page. The book fascinates; it seems always based upon a beautiful, yet most inadequate, conception.

February 20. Many things to remember these last weeks: Mr. Whittier's visit, and my almost daily glimpses of him, and talks with him, — a friendship that grows more satisfactory as the years deepen life. Separateness of life makes communion of thought almost truer and more inspiring than when people live near each other, and frequently meet. I have more admiration and reverence for such a man, from having found a higher standard in life for myself from which to look across and up to him. I think everybody who has largeness of character like his needs perspective; juxtaposition is not acquaintance.

April 27. The weeks pass too busily for record; also I have not been well. Read with Miss H—— Maurice's "Gospel of the Kingdom," Fairbairn's "Studies in the Life of Christ," Neander, "Life of Christ;" and came to Maurice's "Lectures on the Gospel of St. John," which is left for future study. . . . A clearer light has come, and yet the sadness of not living wholly in the light: the bitterness of error and failure!

I will not be morbid; I know that there is always a better self than myself, waiting to be set free. But the riddles of life are perplexing. Who are we? What are we struggling for?

I think Maurice one of the most illuminating writers I ever knew. He looks into a truth, and you see what he sees, if you see anything.

This stirring up of theological questions at Andover is a phenomenon of the time; a movement towards a simpler holding of truth, and let us trust a greater honesty in us all in our statements of belief. Opinions change, but faith lives in the heart of the truth, not in its outward expression. I wish some formulas could be laid aside, and that we could come into a real unity of faith.

May 26. Closing days of a lovely visit at Melrose, at the house of two of the most delightful people, — a true home.

The woods close the house in around my window, and the birds sing close by. A squirrel has fearlessly come in to visit me once or twice; a flying squirrel, they say it is. The people I am with show me how beautiful it is to live truth, justice, and sympathy. They belong to no Church, but their lives are most beautifully harmonized with the spirit of Him who was, and is, the expression of God's love to man. When with them I almost feel as if it were better not to profess religion in churches, — this living testimony is so far beyond what most Christians can show; but then I remember that it is because God in Christ is in the world, because the divinity has revealed itself in humanity, that they are what they are. How else have truth, honor, tenderness, and unselfishness, been kept alive in the human hearts, but by that revelation of the one life as the divine standard? And if the churches were all forsaken now, we should see a sad falling off from among us of such people as these, for most of us need constant reminders that we are the children of God. We need the Word, the coming together, the loving, uniting memories of Him who is our life.

Longfellow and Emerson gone from us before the opening of spring! It is strange to think of New England without them. But they are part of its life, forever. . . .

Though Miss Larcom was progressing in her knowledge of the Episcopal Church, she felt no nearer an entrance into that body. She was willing to enjoy the services at Trinity Church, but she did not want Mr. Brooks to think, because of her constant attendance, she had any thoughts of confirmation. So in 1884 she wrote him a letter, stating her position, which he most cordially accepted, writing her in reply what he considered the advantages of her attitude.

233 Clarendon Street, Boston, March 20, 1884.

My dear Miss Larcom, — My delay in answering your letter does not mean that I was not deeply interested in it, and very glad to get it. It only means that I have been too busy to write calmly about anything, and even now I write mainly to say how glad I shall be if some time or other we can quietly talk over what you have written. For the present, however, let me only say, that I accept most cordially the position which you describe for yourself. I am content that our Church should be a helpful friend to one who has been living among quite different associations, and who does not think it best to come into closer personal connection with her. If God means that there should ever be a closer association of life between you and the Episcopal Church, He will make it plain in due time. It is not bad, perhaps, that among the special connections with particular bodies of Christians which come in our lives, there should be one period in which, from the very breaking of our associations with the bodies of Christians, we are able to realize more directly our relation to the body of Christ. Perhaps this is such a time for you. If it is, and whether it is or not, may you find more and more of His light and help, and if anything that I can do, or that Trinity Church can do, is ever a source of happiness or strength to you, I know that you will be sure that I am very glad. With kindest wishes, always,

I am yours most sincerely,

PHILLIPS BROOKS.

CHAPTER X.

UNDERCURRENTS.

1884–1889.

TO MISS S. H. WARD.

January 1, 1884.

Dear Susie Ward, — Something has just brought you to mind; I saw your address in print in an almanac, and I felt like sending a New Year's greeting to the schoolgirl I knew — *was* it thirty years ago?

I am very fond of those dear girls of mine, though I seldom see them, and would like to send a New Year's greeting to them all.

Ever your friend,

Lucy Larcom.

TO THE SAME.

Beverly, Mass., January 15, 1884.

My dear Susie, — It is so pleasant to take up the threads of an old friendship again! It always reassures me of the hereafter of souls, that even here after long intervals, we find ourselves still at home with those who had slipped away from us apparently. They are really still in their place, and we are sure of them and know where to find them.

I have had many changes since we were much together, but life is the same good gift of the Lord I always knew it to be, only more wonderful as one gets deeper into it.

Always yours,

LUCY LARCOM.

TO J. G. WHITTIER.

WOLFVILLE, NOVA SCOTIA,
August 21, 1884.

MY DEAR FRIEND, — I am moved to write to you from here, where I sit looking out upon the Basin of Minas, and Grand Pré itself, the mud of which latter I have been trying to remove from my dress, though I suppose I ought to let it stay spattered with poetic associations!

Yesterday we were taken to drive through the Valley of the Gaspereau, a lovely region, under perfect cultivation, — and so on, over the old dikes of Grand Pré, where we stood upon the site of the old church, and saw the cellar of what was supposed to be the priest's house, close by the church.

The people here think they know where Evangeline's father lived, and just where Basil the blacksmith had his forge, — so mixed are our illusions with our historic certainties! I find myself believing in Evangeline as a real maiden, one who once lived and suffered on this very soil, and I gathered a daisy and a wild rose for you, which her hand might have plucked, instead of mine, as a memorial of her lost home.

Miss J—— and I are stopping at the village doctor's. Mrs. Fitch, who keeps his house, takes a very few boarders. His orchard is loaded with apples and pears, and his garden opens out on the meadow close upon the first dike built by the French Acadians. We are finding the hottest weather of the season, and are glad not to be in any city just now.

We had a pleasant sail to Halifax — the sea as smooth as glass, and so no excuse for sickness. I had friends in Halifax, who took us to the citadel and the park, the latter the finest I ever saw, because left chiefly to nature: just woods of pine and spruce, overlooking the harbor, which I can well believe to be what the Nova Scotians claim for it — the most beautiful harbor in the world.

We go the last of the week to Annapolis and Digby, and home by the way of Mt. Desert, which I have never visited.

I go from there to Bethel, to spend September, — read my proof — and escape hay-fever — (as I hope!).

You are often spoken of here, and by those who wish you would visit the place. The journey is a long one, and I suppose, as I tell them, that you would not feel like taking it. But there is a charm about the people and the region which can only be felt by being here, — everybody seems very intelligent, and very hospitable, — no extreme poverty anywhere, that I can see.

Thine always,

LUCY LARCOM.

TO PHILLIPS BROOKS.

12 Concord Square, March 26, 1885.

Dear Mr. Brooks, — I called at the chapel yesterday afternoon, but others were waiting to see you, and it was getting late in the day, so I did not stay. I had, indeed, no good excuse for taking your time; but it would have been a great pleasure to speak to you, after my winter's imprisonment with illness.

It is only within a week or two that I have come to Boston, or been out to church at all. I have enjoyed, almost to pain, the few services I have attended, for I am not sure that I hold myself in the right manner towards God's people, with whom I so fully sympathize in spirit. I wonder if I really am in the Church! My childish consecration was sincere; I entered the communion of the sect in which I was baptized and brought up, from an earnest longing to come nearer to Christ, — a desire which has grown with me through all the years; only now it reaches out beyond all names and groupings, towards the whole Communion of Saints in Him. Nothing less than this is the real Church to me. Some narrowness I find in every denomination, and this distresses and repels me, so that I cannot tell where I belong. Yet when I go to Trinity Church, I feel myself taken possession of, borne upward on the tide of loving loyalty to Christ; and I know that it has not been well for me to live apart from my kindred.

I wish I could find myself among the group who consecrate themselves to-night: but, as you once said to me, if that were the way for me, it would be made plain. And I shall consider Trinity as home, whenever I am in Boston.

I did have one little request to make, — it was liberty to use some paragraphs from your printed sermons in a compilation which I may prepare this year. I shall take it that I have permission, unless forbidden.

Faithfully yours,

LUCY LARCOM.

TO ——

December 3, 1885.

I heard Canon Farrar preach and lecture. He is not remarkable, it seems to me, except for his moral and spiritual earnestness, but that is remarkable, as men go. I liked his lecture, for it will help to foster a good feeling between us two brother nations of the English race. England and America ought to feel themselves one. . . .

When the summer came, Miss Larcom always looked forward with pleasure to her mountain-homes, of which she had a number, in New Hampshire and Maine. The hills gave her rest; and the beauty of the views, with the grand distances, suggesting freedom and the thought of being above the common level, gave her inspiration for her work. Each year she tried to visit the various points she loved — Ossipee Park, The Notch, Bethlehem, Moosilauke, Bethel, Centre Harbor, and Berlin Falls. Bethel fascinated her with its sight of the Androscoggin and its majestic elms, and the view of Mt. Moriah and some of the Presidential Range, — Madison, Adams, and Washington. At Mr. John Russell's Riverside Cottage she was always welcome; and back of the house, on the crest of the mountain, was a little glen, shaded by evergreens, in which she used to sit and read, called "Miss Larcom's Retreat." Sitting on the low bench, in this nook, she wrote the poem "On the Ledge:" —

> "Here is shelter and outlook, deep rest and wide room;
> The pine woods behind, breathing balm out of gloom;
> Before, the great hills over vast levels lean, —
> A glory of purple, a splendor of green.
> As a new earth and heaven, ye are mine once again,
> Ye beautiful meadows and mountains of Maine."

She always enjoyed Ossipee Park, with its wonderful brook, "set in the freshness of perfect green," and watched it widen into pools and leap into cascades. She wrote of it, "Ah! this is the sort of retreat for friends who like to meet or separate within the sound of a voice which surely wins them together again side by side."

Bethlehem, besides giving her freedom from hay-fever, was always "the beautiful." Moosilauke was her favorite summit. From these places she generally wrote charming letters to the Portland "Transcript," which its readers will remember, and others may judge of by the following from Wood-Giant's Hill, Centre Harbor.

"There is a peculiar charm in New Hampshire hill scenery just at this season, before the roses have faded, or the hay is mown, or the bobolinks have ceased singing among the clover blossoms, and while the midsummer-tide is rolling up over all, and blending all in haze and heat, — a mingling of freshness and ripeness that is indescribably lovely. One should surely be among the hills before the Fourth of July, to catch the best of their beauty, as well as to escape the dust and distractions of the patriotic anniversary.

"To sit at a western window and look off upon the Beulah-like landscape, slope upon slope of rolling, forest-crowned hills ascending towards bluer heights which lose themselves among dim lines of half-revealed higher horizons — to feel the air sweeping across from the softly-blended infinite spaces, over pine woods and fields in full flower — to breathe it all in like the odor of some divine nectar — is there anything like it in the whole year, except at the meeting point of June and July, and in such a region as this. For we know that there are lakes all around us, sleeping unseen in the midsummer haze, and we know that the invisible mountains lie just beyond those lovely ascending distances before us.

"And so, when a sweeter waft of coolness refreshes every sense, and we ask with wonder what makes it so sweet, the answer seems borne onward with its very breath: —

"'The gale informs us, laden with the scent.'

"It brings us the spice of pine woods and the clear drip of ice-cold waterfalls ; the breath of pond lilies and sweet-brier and unmown scented grasses, clover-tops and mountain-tops, blended in one draught; and that delicate bubble of song which rises from the meadows, the faint farewell chorus of summer birds that seem loth to go, makes the full cup overflow with musical foam.

"I saw the sun drop last evening — its magnified reflection, rather — into the larger Lake Asquam, like a ball of crimson flame. The sun itself went down, hot and red, into a band of warm mist that hung over the hills. The 'Wood Giant' stood above me audibly musing. His twilight thoughts were untranslatable, but perhaps the wood-thrushes understood, for they sent up their mystical chant from the thickets below, in deep harmony with the music of his boughs.

"The higher summits have not unveiled themselves yet, not even Cardigan or Mount Israel. Steaming across the lake from Wolfboro' three sunsets since, it seemed to me that there was a compensation in this invisibility of the loftier hills. Only Red Hill and the Ossipee Range were to be seen ; and they loomed up in huge grandeur, asserting themselves to be, as they are, the dominant guardians of Winnipiseogee. It is seldom that the Beautiful Lake loses them from sight."

TO MRS. S. I. SPALDING.

CENTRE HARBOR, N. H., October 7, 1885.

. . . I have had my "outing" at Bethlehem; I went there hardly able to sit up during the journey, but gained strength at once, and am well now.

I stayed there more than four weeks, and enjoyed it much. Mr. Howells and family were at the next house, and I saw them several times. Bethlehem is a very public place. I found a good deal of calling and visiting going on. But the house life was delightful.

I spent last week at Ossipee Park, the loveliest spot in New England, I think.

I am here for a week or more, at the place where Mr. Whittier was in the summer. Mrs. Sturtevant is an old friend of mine, and her housekeeping leaves nothing to be desired. You would like the place and it is easily accessible, — only a mile back of Centre Harbor. Mr. Whittier's poem, "The Wood Giant," was written here. You can see the tree above others, ten miles across the lake, at Ossipee Park — it is down in the pasture, a little way from this house, looking towards sunset over the lake. . . .

TO J. G. WHITTIER.

HOTEL BYRON,
BOSTON, April 23, 1886.

MY DEAR FRIEND, — I have been in and about Boston for the past three weeks, and of late have been interested in this new study of Theosophy, which so many are looking into. I have wondered how you regard it.

What I most enjoy about it is the larger horizons it opens upon our true spiritual sight, — glimpses only, it is true, — but we could not bear more than that, doubtless. And the moral and spiritual truth it unfolds and inculcates is of the loftiest. It harmonizes so entirely with the highest Christianity, no believer in that can find cause for cavil. And yet, it is far behind the spirit of Christianity, as we have it from the Divine Teacher's lips and life; in that the common mind is shut out from a clear comprehension of its meaning. "The simplicity that is in Christ" is the true gospel, whatever wisdom beside this may be given to sages and seekers. The gospel for the poor and the ignorant is the gospel for us all.

And I suppose those that go farthest into these other deep secrets are the humblest. Spiritual pride is indeed pronounced the greatest of all sins by these, and by Christian souls.

But how beautiful it is to know that truth is one, and that life is one, and that all over the world, and through all the ages, men are entering into and sharing the great inheritance!

I may find much that I cannot accept, but what of that, if I am brought nearer to the heart of humanity, in its fraternal aspirations towards the Father of our spirits!

Faithfully thy friend, LUCY LARCOM.

233 CLARENDON STREET,
BOSTON, December 28, 1886.

DEAR MISS LARCOM, — I cannot let your kind note pass without at least a word of gratitude and welcome. It is good to know that you are in Boston again, and that I may sometimes speak to you on Sundays. I should be sorry indeed to think that the winter would pass without letting me, somewhere, sometime, come to more familiar friendly talk with you. You will find me the chance, I hope, either by coming here, or letting me know where I may come to you.

At any rate, I am glad that you are here, and I send you my best New Year's wishes.

I do not want you to think that I am aspiring to poetry. "The Little Town of Bethlehem" was written more than twenty years ago, for a Christmas service of my Sunday school in Philadelphia. It has been printed in hymn-books since, and sung at a good many Christmases, and where the newspapers find it, all of a sudden, I do not know!

Ever faithfully your friend,
PHILLIPS BROOKS.

It has been stated that Miss Larcom was barely able to support herself by her writings. She realized, like many another author, that Mr. Whittier's words were true when he wrote her that "the hardest way of earning bread and butter in this world is to coin one's brains, as an author, into cash, or spin them into greenbacks." She could, however, do very well, so long as her health was good. In addition to the copyright on her books, she received payment from the magazines for her work, — "St. Nicholas" sometimes gave her fifty dollars for an article. "Harper's" and the "Independent" paid her the same rates as they did to "H. H." She also contributed to "Wide Awake," the "Christian Union," the "Congregationalist," and to many minor papers, like the "Cottage Hearth." But she was subject to severe attacks of illness, which rendered her, for the time, incapable of writing. Then it was that her friends came forward to aid her; any assistance, however, she was loth to accept. This unwillingness to receive help gave rise to an interesting scene between herself and Mr. Whittier. At one time, her strength and resources had been reduced by illness. She was lying upon her couch when Mr. Whittier came, and, seating himself beside her, said, "Now, Lucy, this is altogether too bad."

"What is too bad?"

"Why, that thee should work for the world all thy days, and then lie here, worrying about expenses."

"I don't worry. The Lord has always taken care of me."

"But, Lucy, thee ought to worry. The Lord has made thee capable of caring for thyself. Why not be more practicable? I have done something about this."

"I knew you had, as soon as this talk began.

Now, I thank you, but I will not touch one cent of the money you collect."

"Don't be foolish. Thee will; and thee must not waste thy remaining strength in rebellion."

A compromise was made by her taking a pension of a hundred dollars a year, from a Quaker Home, in Philadelphia, and a few annual subscriptions — one from Mr. George W. Childs.

TO J. G. WHITTIER.

HOTEL BYRON, BERKELEY ST.,
BOSTON, MASS., February 4, 1887.

MY DEAR FRIEND, — I have been away two days, and on returning, find thy note and the enclosed check for one hundred dollars. A greater surprise could not have awaited me.

And, curiously enough, I had been amusing myself just before, with the thought of the great fortunes rolling about the world, without ever so much as touching me! And I had said to myself that the Great Disposer of all these things, who is also my Father, doubtless had a purpose in it, — perhaps that I was to prove to the very end that life could be very cheerful and comfortable without much money, and with unremitting effort to earn a moderate living, so long as my strength should hold out.

And I felt like acquiescing gratefully, happy in my restored health, in my interest in my work, and in doing and being all that it is in me to do and to be for others, — for life does look every day larger and deeper and more beautiful in its possibilities, even this one small life of mine, in this world of God's. I think I was rather in danger of looking down on the millionaires, and pitying them for their heavier burdens of responsibility.

I always feel rich when I feel well, and I was not conscious of a present want, although I knew my purse was getting light, and I was not sure whether I could afford to stay in Boston through the winter, but now I see that I can, for I shall take your advice, and keep the check.

I suppose I should never have consented to have my name used, as one who needed assistance, but I have great confidence in your wisdom, and if you thought it right, I could not object. But you know that I have never suffered from want, and that I am able to work, although three-score.

The only wish I have ever had in connection with money, is for the freedom it might give me to choose my work, and the place where I should live. When I can do that, I don't know that I shall have any further desire, for myself. And if I really need that, God will give it to me.

If Mr. Childs has really sent the money to *me*, I must thank him for it, and I will do so, if you will kindly send me his address. You see how ignorant I am about our good rich people, when I don't know whether to address him as "Mr." or "Esq." or write with Quaker plainness! You said, "Philadelphia." Is that enough, without street or number?

I thank thee sincerely for all the kind thoughts that this matter implies on thy part. And I feel more and more assured that the silver and the gold belong to God, and that He spends it where He will. If He puts it into Mr. Childs' hand for me, I will not refuse it — not from any good man's hand. Only please remember that thee must not let people think I am poor, when I am not. Shall we not see thee before long?

Gratefully yours,

LUCY LARCOM.

One of Miss Larcom's greatest pleasures was the visits she was able to make to her congenial friends. Not being tied by family cares, it was possible for her to accept some of the many invitations she constantly received from those who loved her. Her presence in a household was like a peaceful influence, for she had the delightful gift of being an agreeable guest. Always sympathetic, never intruding into the privacy of family matters, reticent about her troubles, and eager to impart her joys, with a fund of humor always at hand, she made a charming companion; and her visit was always remembered as an event in the year. There are many homes that have had the privilege of entertaining her, and receiving something from the close contact with her personality. One of her hostesses, Mrs. James Guild, of Roxbury, in whose house she used to enjoy hours of Plato study, and where the last few years of her life she found rest, says, "In passing the library, I often looked through the portières, to behold the presence in the room, — the white, peaceful face, that seemed to wear a halo. She would have three or four books at once on her knee, and look up smiling to ask, 'Am I not greedy? I don't know which of these to read first! I do love books, but not better than friends; when you are at leisure, I am ready to sit with you.'"

TO MRS. S. I. SPALDING.

WILLIAMSTOWN, MASS., October 10, 1887.

. . . I came here, through Lake George and Saratoga, last Friday. I am visiting at President Carter's, my old friend, who has a charming family and home. The town itself is most beautiful, and I have been driving about among the Berkshire Hills, finding them no less enjoyable for what I have seen of the Adirondacks.

President Carter is at present away on business. A case of possible hazing is one of the most trying — the facts are so hard to get at. The spirit of this college is entirely opposed to such things. He is also a corporate member of the American Board. I do not sympathize with the turn affairs have taken. It looks to me like a long step backward. It cannot be that a disputed theological point is to settle the world's salvation. And the inquisitorial spirit tends so entirely to bitterness and harsh judgment; it proves itself foreign to the spirit of Christ.

May God reveal himself to these benighted theologians!

TO J. G. WHITTIER.

BEVERLY, MASS., April 24, 1888.

MY DEAR FRIEND, — Yesterday I returned to Beverly, having done something quite uncommon, for me, — taken a trip to the Jerseys. I went on urgent invitation from old pupils and school-friends at Wheaton Seminary, who gave a breakfast at Hotel Brunswick, New York.

I met a good many people I was glad to see, and made most of my visit at Mr. Ward's, of the "Independent." His sister, who keeps house for him, at Newark, is a former pupil of mine.

Then I had an invitation from a schoolmate at Monticello, Illinois, who lives at Orange, New Jersey, and I stayed there several days. I went over New York and Brooklyn by the bridge and the elevated railway, but scarcely touched the metropolis. However, I saw my old friends, and a good many new people, and had a pleasant time.

And now, I am urgently invited to my old Illinois seminary, in June, when it has its semi-centennial anniversary. I am afraid I shall have to go, as my Minnesota sister seconds the motion, and she expects to move to California, another year. What a moving world it is! . . .

The "New England Girlhood," published in 1889, was at once a success. Few facts of Miss Larcom's life had been generally known up to this time; there had been, however, interesting biographical sketches printed from time to time, notably Mrs. A. D. T. Whitney's sketch, in "American Women of Note," and her own article, in the "Atlantic Monthly," with the title "Among Lowell Mill-Girls." But in this book she took her friends into her confidence, and showed such genuineness of feeling, and love for her modest beginnings in the old town of Beverly, with its lanes, its woods, and its seacoast, that her description stirred up the memory of similar days in the thought of New England people, at home, and in distant parts of the country. This account of her youth contains the best elements of her thought and life, in a story, charming for its simplicity and truthful portraiture of New England homes before any of the modern changes had taken place, — those changes that introduced stoves and shut up the great fireplaces, that substituted for the stage-coach the horse and electric car, put clocks on the mantelpiece, and relegated to the junk-shops the "tin kitchens" and the three-legged "trivet." Its homely incident and the sincerity of its religious sentiment render it an excellent book to put into the hands of young girls; by reading it they are brought into connection with the refined and vigorous girlhood of an actual life. One critic remarked, "If there could be more biography like this, there would be less call for fiction." Miss Larcom received numerous letters of thanks for having written the book. A gentleman sent her a check, as an evidence of his satisfaction. An aged man wrote,

— "If it was written for the young, it certainly was for the old. I am now eighty-five years old and never was more delighted." Mr.. Whittier sent his approval: "I am reading the book for the second time, with increased pleasure; I recall my first meeting with thee at Lowell, after thy return from the West."

That she enjoyed these tokens of appreciation, this letter indicates.

TO MRS. S. I. SPALDING.

214 Columbus Avenue,
Saturday evening, December 28, 1889.

My dear Friend, — I have just come in and read Mrs. S——'s letter, which I return. Her enthusiasm inspires me just as I like to be inspired. I felt in writing the book that I was just entering into my past life, and taking my friends with me. I did not feel that I was making a "literary effort," but just taking a little journey backward.

I appreciate the readers who will simply go along with me, as Mrs. S—— does. I am glad to give myself to those who understand the gift, and I would like to find more in myself for them, if I could. It is just like taking hold of hands all round, these pleasant acknowledgments that come to me. It is *our* life that we are enjoying together. . . .

Mr. Brooks sent one of his short, characteristic notes, thanking her for "A New England Girlhood."

233 Clarendon Street,
Boston, December 9, 1889.

My dear Miss Larcom, — I have never been a Yankee girl, and yet I felt that I recognized every picture in what I read, and I have read it all.

To hear of the American First Class Book again was like a breeze out of my childhood!

And I hope all the girls are reading it, and catching the flavor of its healthy spirit.

At any rate, I thank you for it, and I am yours most sincerely, Phillips Brooks.

CHAPTER XI.

MEMBERSHIP IN THE EPISCOPAL CHURCH.

The longing for a religious home asserted itself in Miss Larcom's life, and the thought came to her that she was not testifying to her deep love for her Master, by withholding herself from active membership in some Church of Christ. In her diary, where she wrote with great freedom her inmost feelings, there are passages which indicate discontent with her negative position. She was being forced to a conclusion: —

"I must decide for myself whether the Church is a reality to me; whether, in the visible Church, working for it, and with it, I can be more useful than I should be, floating on still, trying to accommodate myself to circumstances, and to harmonize myself with the best in everything, without any special ties. Having lived outside the Church so long, I have a great longing for a closer sympathy and working together with others. But whether it can be with my old Congregational friends, I am not certain. It would be better to stay with them, identified with their name and work, if I can do it from my heart, but not if I am called upon to say anything that I do not believe."

While in this state of uncertainty, the Church was gradually making its way into her life. She looked forward to each Sunday, with eagerness; and the message from the day's sermon she either put in her diary, or conveyed, by means of letters, to her little crippled friend, Elsie L——.

The Church-Year, with its sacred anniversaries, became very dear to her. In her diary, there is a record referring to Passion Week, that shows her appreciation of these Church days: "I think it most beautiful to keep these memorial days of the Church, whether we belong to the Episcopal Church or any other. These are the days for all Christians to observe."

April 8, Good Friday. Passion Week has been a revelation to me of the divine history made real. It has seemed to me as if I really followed and faltered with the disciples, in Gethsemane, at the mock trial of Pilate, and through the terrible scenes of the Crucifixion. It is so much to the world, that the Church has kept up the Christian year, with these awful and glorious anniversaries. How often their reality has faded out, when men are left to themselves.

I could thank the Church, almost, for having impressed them so upon her history, that they sometimes seem *hardened* into it! She has never let them become mere idle tales; the life and death of Christ, held so close to her heart, have kept her alive, through all her formalisms.

In the worship, the part taken by the congregation, in responsive readings, prayers, versicles, and Litany, appealed to her. She felt that she was not being preached at through the disguise of a prayer, but that all — minister and people — joined in the praises to God, each with a phrase on his lips and a meditation in his heart. The dignity and orderly arrangement of the services, together with the use of the stately words of the Prayer Book, made her appreciate the beautiful formality of such devotional customs.

Her affections were strengthened by an act which seemed to open a new set of experiences to her. This act was the partaking of the Holy Communion early on Easter Day, in 1887. Mr. Brooks had given notice, inviting to the Lord's Supper any persons who might desire to come, though they belonged to some other branch of the Church of Christ. A friend of Miss Larcom urged her to accept the invitation. The generosity of it fascinated her; the thought of all who loved Jesus, loving Him perhaps in different ways, meeting around the Father's table, was in thorough accord with her own feelings. Going to the service, and taking her place at the altar rail, she received the bread and wine administered in the reverent manner of the Episcopal Church. This one act, in the early morning of Easter day, revealed to her the spiritual meaning of the worship, and seemed to bring her in closest touch with the Master; and afterwards the Church became a different place to her; she was becoming one with it, though she yet had no right to call herself a member. Referring to this Communion, she said, "How free the Lord's table ought to be! and how beautiful it was at that early Communion; the church fragrant and fresh, and glowing with flowers! It seemed like meeting Christ with Mary in the Garden, just as he had risen from the Grave! I do think the Communion service of the church most inreaching and uplifting in its earnestness, its simplicity, its spirituality."

"As I remember this service in the Congregational church, that method seems almost formal in comparison with this. Perhaps there is something in the very movement required, — the person going forward to the table to share the bread and wine, each with the rest, yet each of us receiving them directly from Christ — His own life, to be transfused into ours. There is certainly a clearer meaning in it all to me, whenever I join in the service at Trinity Church.

"The crowd in the church afterwards, who came to the later services and sermon, was also most impressive, filling in even every smallest space in the chancel, among the flowers. The sermon was strong and deep, impressing the thought that life is the one reality, and death and sorrow and sin only partial experiences. Life the ocean, and all these things but ripples on the surface.

"The last thought for the day, — in the evening, — was that injustice never does triumph, however it may seem."

April 22. Emeline's birthday,—the dearest of my sisters — more than a mother to me — now threescore and ten. But I live my child-life over again with her, and our two lives make a glad harmony all through. How much shall we keep of ourselves and our human relations, forever? All that has been real, surely. And so we are mature women and little children together, at once, in the immortal life.

The past week has been one of rather unpleasant experiences, in some ways. The Beverly Farms bribery investigation at the State House has occupied me. Whether bribery or not, great injustice is attempted on my native town, which I love and will defend, so long as I know her to be unmistakably in the right, as she is now.

I have done the little I could, so far; have written for the newspapers, — have sent a letter of request for veto to the governor, — and joined the women of Beverly in a petition to him, to the same effect, and I shall hold myself ready to do more, if needed. But I do trust that our legislature will, of themselves, make the matter right.

April 25. Spring is in the air, even in Boston, although just a week ago to-day we had one of the worst snowstorms of the season.

Yesterday's experience is something not to be forgotten, though unrecordable. There are no words to repeat the spirit's story, when it is taken possession of by the highest influences, and lifted up into the heaven of aspiration and consecration;

when the way is open through sympathy with human souls, and with the Eternal Son, into the Father's heart.

How easy the spiritual life seems, when material things fall into their subordinate places! If it might always be so!

May 20. Still in Boston, interested in many things. People *are* trying to help each other. I have been at the Woman's Industrial Union, have heard Miss Leigh talk of her work in Paris, have talked over the possibilities of better influences for girl-workers in Boston, have listened to Miss Freeman's report of her Student's Aid work at Wellesley College — all so suggestive — so hopeful! What should not the woman of the future be? What may she not be?

> "I saw all women of our race
> Revealed in that one woman's face!"

June 6. Canon Wilberforce and the great temperance meeting at Tremont Temple. A most eloquent man, and he goes to the very root of the matter, — no real temperance without spirituality. "Not drunken with wine, but filled with the Holy Ghost," — he made that infinite contrast clear. His sermon yesterday was most impressive, — from the text, "What seest thou?" It was a Trinity Sunday sermon, and the thought was that in Jesus we see God most perfectly. But emphasis was placed upon the attitude and condition of the soul, for the seeing. It was Canon Wilberforce's first sermon in Boston, and I think this is his first visit to America. It is good to have such neighbors come to see us.

In the afternoon Mr. Brooks spoke from the text, "He that hath the Son hath life." I have seldom heard him speak with more fervor, of what life is, and of the dreadful thing it is to lack life, the life that comes to us and is in us through Christ, — the life of God in human souls. It is his last sermon for the summer, and the text itself is one to keep close at heart all through the year. "Not merely the knowledge of Christ, but Christ Himself with us, we must have," he said: and with the thought comes the suggestion of all true relations of spirit with spirit, the human and the divine interblended, God the soul of our souls and the children one with the Father through the Son. I thank God for what I have found at Trinity Church this winter: I begin to know more what the true Church is, — nothing exclusive or separating, but the coming together of all souls in Christ.

June 12. In Beverly, but not yet acclimated to the stronger sweep of the east winds. They give rheumatic twinges. But the birds sing, and the fresh foliage is shaken out into greenness, the rose acacia and the bridal-wreath spirea run wild in the garden, and the freedom of nature's life revives mine. The thrill of the oriole, — what a jubilation it is, through the Sabbath stillness; it is better than the city in summer time.

Read this morning Phillips Brooks' sermon on

"Visions" and "Tasks," and several others — among them, the "Church of the Living God."

With reference to doctrines, she understood the Church's position. The great facts of Christianity as set forth in the Apostles Creed, she did not doubt; and she liked the comprehensiveness of a Church, admitting those who accept these facts and desire to live a Christian life, and permitting a private opinion on many complicated questions of theology. And yet, with her appreciation for the Church, she could not make up her mind to enter it. There were objections difficult for her to overcome.

These objections were not of a devotional or theological, but of an ecclesiastical character. High-Churchism, including in that term Sacerdotalism, offered a barrier. She felt that, by joining the Church, she would seem to approve of this teaching, and while she was willing to admit the historical fact of Apostolical continuity, she could not accept a theory of Apostolical succession which in any way seemed to exclude from good standing, as Churches, the various religious denominations which she had known and loved. She said, "In the broad idea of Christ's Church, Episcopacy at times seems to me no less sectarian than other 'isms.'" She had too much of the Puritan in her to make any such admissions about the Episcopal Church that would seem to indicate that she felt it was the only Church. Her position, as late as

1890, is very well put, in a letter to Mrs. S. I. Spalding, of Newburyport.

"I do feel nearer a conclusion, such as you would approve, than I ever have yet. I think, sometimes, I can see my way perfectly clear, but old notions are hard to change. Do you think I can take all the Puritanism implied in "A New England Girlhood," into the Church with me? Is it possible to be inside the latter, and yet feel that all the others are Churches, too, and that I am only signifying that I want to be more completely in union with them all, by identifying myself with this one? This is the way I should want to feel and do."

By means of letters and conversations with Mr. Brooks, she saw that it was not necessary for her to give up all her Puritanism, on coming into the Church, nor was she bound to accept the interpretation that some Episcopalians put upon the Sacraments or Orders in the ministry. She learned that the difficulties she was considering were dispelled by the conception of the comprehensiveness of the Church. Mr. Brooks wrote her, concerning a discussion in the Church papers, in which Sacerdotalism was especially rampant: "There is nothing in it, which is not now repeated for the hundredth time. The solution of it all is in the comprehensiveness of the Church, which includes the vast expanse both of breadth and narrowness." In March, 1890, she came to the end of her discussions, and seemed to see the true meaning of the Episcopal

Church, as one method of entering the larger Invisible Church of Christ. She preferred this path to others, but looked upon it as a path, not the end of the journey.

March 1, 1890. The same questionings, — yet a clearer light upon the meaning of the Church has gradually come to me. It is as if there were many doors of entrance into one vast temple, some of them opened a little way, and with much scrutiny from within of applicants for admission; some swung wide with welcome. But there is one united worship inside, only some prefer to group themselves in cloisters or corners; but there is freedom and light for all who will receive them.

The Episcopal Church seems to have several doors of its own, — some wide and some narrow; it is not *the* Church, — only one way of entering Christ's Church. If I can enter it that way, I am already there. And I believe more positively than ever, that we should say, in some distinct, personal way, that Christ is the centre and head of humanity, and that our whole life, earthly and heavenly, is hid in Him.

What belongs to me in Puritanism I shall never lay aside; I could not, if I would. But I do see more of a hope for future unity in the Church service than in any other way; and if I can see therein for myself the perfect freedom of Christ's service, I am ready to make a new profession there. I am waiting only for His guidance, now.

I see more and more how much the writings of Maurice have been to me for the past twenty years. He is continually unfolding my own thoughts to me, — his absolute sincerity is contagious. I want no pretenses, no subterfuges or concessions in the spiritual life. He speaks to me more clearly than almost any audible voice. And his words seem the expression of the mind of Christ.

March 5. My birthday. And the world seems as if it were dimly dawning anew to me. Everything in my life has taken a touch of awe, — of strangeness.

I do not know that there is any new gladness in the decision I made yesterday, to be "confirmed" at Trinity Church, but there is a settled feeling that may grow into happiness. I can say that my "heart is fixed," and my life will be firmer and more settled, for having found a place for itself. The church itself seemed a different and more beautiful place, as I sat there and listened to the story of the Woman of Samaria, and of the separateness of souls in consecrated work. "Meat to eat that ye know not of," the doing of God's will, — the hidden manna and the white stone, with the new name known only to him who receives it. Yes, this one little decision has opened closed doors to me already — everything looks sacred.

March 20. Last night I knelt in the chancel at Trinity Church, and received, with many others, the benediction of consecrated hands; and to-day I can think of myself as avowedly in the visible

Church once more. I have been in a false position all these years, — I see it now. It does mean something to name the name of Christ in the presence of His people, as one of their company. I have not been an unbeliever, ever; He has been dear to me always, and most real to my heart.

It was tranquillizing, to be bending there with all that young life, — (no other older life), the snow falling without, soft and white as doves' wings, and the quiet consecration filling all hearts within. I was not wholly happy; I have had too many struggles with myself, and misapprehension between my own heart and others, perhaps, to feel glad or uplifted, — but I was calm and thankful, and felt the atmosphere of blessing surrounding us all.

It is good to have taken this position; I shall feel stronger and richer in life and spirit for it, I trust and believe.

The few words of Mr. Brooks this morning at the church seemed to carry out the spirit of last night's service. We climb up the great mountain-tops, he said, but we cannot live there, though we may keep their inspiration within us. But the high table-lands which we have gained by long gradual ascent, — we can live and breathe there; and can grow hopeful in the broad outlook before us. Such are the consecrations of life to which we have grown step by step, out of which greater developments are to open for us, and above which the loftier summits are always overhanging.

March 26. The thought that has been with me

most these few days is that consecration means service: that it is not for one's self alone, — not the mere endeavor after personal holiness, — but to give the life into which we enter to all other lives we can reach. (John xvii. 18, 19.) The spirit of these words of Christ is the true setting apart of life, for the sake of all human lives.

The chapter for to-day — the going forth of Joshua into Canaan after that glorious Nebo-Vision of Moses, is full of suggestions for me. I have not yet possessed my whole life, none of us have, but we go forward courageously into it, in the name of the Lord.

We have sketched, chiefly in her own words, for they have a greater significance, the history of a religious woman, finding her way into the Kingdom of Christ through the doorway of the Episcopal Church. She was a catholic, broad-minded Christian, and she became satisfied with the doctrine and worship of the Church. She looked upon it as one branch of the Church of God, but she also acknowledged other branches; it became as much a home to her as it was possible for any Church to be. She grew to love it, but the ideal and Invisible Church was ever before her mind.

The religious history of her life is like that of many others — those who have become dissatisfied with a theology made up of men's opinions, and who seek light and life in the personality of Jesus. There are many persons to-day, with natures capable of spiritual insight, who have been educated to appreciate the best in our literature, who believe in righteousness, — people with poetry in them, and a delicate sense of fitness and dignity, who are thinking of the Episcopal Church as a religious home. To such persons, a progress similar to that of Miss Larcom can be effected only by the Church emphasizing those qualities which attracted her. These characteristics of the Church may be summarized as the spirituality, the breadth, and the magnanimity of the Church.

Prominent through all the services, the various organized forms of church work, the observances of festivals and seasons, must be the spiritual idea for which they all stand. This spiritual idea is the bringing of the individual soul into such relations with Jesus that it will find its truest self in Him and through Him, find its greatest activity in reaching other souls. This great aim is frequently lost sight of, because the Churches are so often business establishments for the collection of money, and the successful management of organizations. But there are souls longing to be fed, and these should be remembered when the church seasons come, by the administration of Sacraments as the simple offering of nourishment to those who need it, not with the theological accompaniments of argument, but in the sacredness of dependence on Christ, as in the first Easter communion of Lucy Larcom, at Trinity Church.

There is no need to elaborate the ideas of the

breadth, or magnanimity of the Church; for, in this day of vigorous thought and reconstruction of older doctrines, both of these characteristics would seem to commend themselves, on their simple announcement: for who is it that longs for the narrowness of a "Westminster Confession" or even the mild bondage of "The Thirty-Nine Articles"? And who is it that has sufficient effrontery to unchurch the millions who are trying in their own ways to serve their Lord? That there is such narrowness in the Episcopal Church no one can deny; it is in opposition to this that it must present itself to the world, as a comprehensive and tolerant Church.

Lucy Larcom, a Puritan, seized upon the vital truths of the Episcopal Church. If these are kept before the people, this Church, as a part of the kingdom of Christ, may hope to have a large influence in the development of American Christianity.

CHAPTER XII.

LAST YEARS.

Miss Larcom was loved in Beverly. The townspeople were justly proud of her, and they always welcomed her sweet face into their homes. She was interested in the Town Improvement Society, and once, at one of its entertainments, she read two or three of her poems. When there was an effort made to secure Prospect Hill for a public park, she sent some appropriate lines to the local paper, hoping to influence opinion. Her public spirit, as shown in her letters and diaries, was also active in her life, and she joined, according to her opportunities, in such affairs as could receive aid from her pen, and the townspeople were gratified by her contributions to the village life.

The success in literature of a Beverly boy made her happy. When Mr. George E. Woodberry entered the company of American poets by the publishing of the "North Shore Watch," a volume containing the triumphant ode, "My Country," not unworthy of comparison with Lowell's "Commemoration Ode," and the strong sonnets, "At Gibraltar," and the classic "Agathon," she was one of the first to send him her appreciation.

TO GEORGE EDWARD WOODBERRY.

214 COLUMBUS AVENUE,
BOSTON, February 18, 1889.

DEAR MR. WOODBERRY, — I have just been reading your poems, and have been so much moved by them that I wanted at once to tell you how deeply they appeal to me. Most of our modern verse, — and I include my own, — is too superficially lyrical, the measure often muffles the meaning, — the thought flies off through the sound. In yours, the music and the meaning unfold together, always hinting the deeper chords half awakened beneath. The feeling of the unexpressed and the inexpressible infinite — that which is at the source of everything real — that which is life itself, is in your poetry, as in almost no other modern poetry that I have read.

The "Transcript" compares it with Clough's. I delight in Clough, but I do not like comparisons of this kind. You strike different chords, and I believe that you have greater possibilities than he. What touches me especially is the high purity of emotion which is yet as human as it is holy. This is rare, even in great poetry. As I read some lines, it seemed as if my soul were weeping for joy at their beauty.

"Agathon" I wanted to read over again as soon as I had finished it. Indeed, I shall want to turn to it often, for a breath of the pure poetic ether. I do not know a greater poem of its kind since

"Comus." Page 42, and from 59 onward, Milton might have been proud to write. They appeal to all that nobler part of us that lives beneath the shows of things; and I am glad that so young a poet as you begins his song so nobly. I am proud, too, that you are a Beverly boy, as I am a Beverly woman. But for that, I might not have ventured to write so freely. I have not room to write all I want to say, but I must mention the "Christ Scourged," which seems to me wonderful in its strength of sympathetic expression. It would give me great pleasure to meet you. If you are staying in town, I wish you would call here some evening.

Truly yours,

LUCY LARCOM.

In preparing a new edition of "Songs of Three Centuries," she included among the additions, a poem by Dr. Solis-Cohen, "I Know that My Redeemer Liveth," and also, "The Crowing of the Red Cock," by Emma Lazarus. In the course of the correspondence, Dr. Solis-Cohen wrote so frankly, giving his feelings about Christ from an intelligent Jewish standpoint, that she answered in a similar vein, stating clearly her idea of the relations that should exist between the Jew and Christian. Dr. Solis-Cohen had written: "No professed Christian can exceed many Jews in love for the pure and lofty character of Jesus, and we can readily accept that character, as a manifestation of God in man, while we decline to accept the superstructure of the Church."

TO DR. SOLOMON SOLIS-COHEN.

BEVERLY, MASS., October 18, 1890.

DR. S. SOLIS-COHEN: —

Dear Sir, — The proof of your poem is just received, — and I have put your corrections away so carefully that I cannot at this moment lay my hand upon them; so I will ask you to correct the copy and send it to the printers as soon as convenient. I will tell them to wait for it.

The magazine with the poem in it is received — beautiful and graceful I find the latter. I wish the additions to the "Songs" were not limited — but the publishers do not wish to enlarge the volume too much. We shall have two poems by Emma Lazarus; one of them Mr. Whittier tells me he considers her best — "The Crowing of the Red Cock."

Your letter interests me exceedingly. I grew up under the influence of old-fashioned Puritanism, and from it drew the idea that Jew and Christian were really one, only they did not understand each other.

Children do construct their own theology oftener than is thought, I believe. The Puritan was like the Hebrew in many ways, most of all in his firm hold of moral distinctions, in his belief in the One God as the God of righteousness and truth.

Certainly no one ever insisted upon obedience to

the law more positively than Christ himself. We Christians do believe in Him as the human manifestation of God: that is the one distinctive element of our faith.

All sorts of strange doctrines have been built up about this idea.

I care for none of them, but rest upon what is to me a spiritual certainty — "Truly this *is* the Son of God."

I emphasize the "*is*" because to me that visible life was only one phase of His eternal presence in and with humanity. To me He is "the living Lord" — the Spirit bearing witness to our spirits of their own immortal meaning; and so "the Resurrection and the Life."

But His life has no spiritual power over ours, unless it teaches us divine love — unless we live in that love which He came to unveil.

Christians have miserably failed of this — in their treatment of each other as well as of the Jews, but it is because they have not received the spirit of their Master.

I thank you sincerely for writing to me so freely, and I thank you for having written the poem enclosed, which bears the same message to me as a Christian, that it does to you as a Jew. I should like to know more of Emma Lazarus. Her early death was a loss to all lovers of true poetry.

Very truly yours,

LUCY LARCOM.

The ecstacy of a sudden realization of religious truth sometimes overcame her in the summer mornings, and her heart uttered itself fervently in prayer, as will be seen in the following extracts from her diary.

July 5, 1890. I awoke with a strange joy as of some new revelation, that seemed sounding through my soul, with the words, "Lift up your heads, O ye gates, and be ye lift up, ye everlasting doors, and the King of Glory shall come in!"

Is it a new entering in of life and love at all the doors of my nature? doors that I have left closed and overgrown, perhaps? Come in, O Life, O Truth, O Love, by whatever gate thou wilt, — in whatever form thou wilt! Only make me ready to receive thee, and to go with thee through the gates into the freedom of thy universe!

August 3. Now I see life more clearly in all its bearings, its dangers, and its hopes, — its earthly and heavenly unity. It is almost like beginning a new childhood in the Kingdom of Heaven. All things centre themselves in Christ, the living, spiritual Christ, who is the Life, the Reality, the Person, who makes us real to each other through the eternal union with the Father. Nature is alive. Nothing is dead that the heart of God has touched. And human beings seem so near and dear!

I think of those who have gone, of my sisters Louisa and Charlotte, of my mother, of all the friends whom I see no more, but who have made part of my true life. They seem more alive than when here; my communion is with them and with all the living to-day.

August 6. This morning, with the opening of my windows on the white floating clouds of summer, and the warm hillside, softened with the mist of coming showers, a song and a hymn arose in my thoughts: —

O Thou Eternal Loveliness, — I am part of Thee, or I am not at all! Nature is the expression of Thee, but yet more is this human life of mine. Because I am, and can feel and see this beauty, — feel it as a part of my own life and soul, I know that Thou art — the Divine One in whom all that is immortal of me is enfolded, and from whom it is unfolded. How can Thy being be questioned by one who has had a single glimpse of the beauty of this Thy world? It is such happiness to feel that I am part of it all, because I belong to Thee! Yet I should never have known the spirit of it all, never should have understood the secret, except through the Son, who has brought Thy children back to their spiritual home in Thee. In Him the evil of earth is conquered, and the good of earth is shown also to be the good of heaven. To be of one spirit with Him, the Perfect Love and the Infinite Loveliness, is to belong to the Whole, and so to Thee. And so there can be no losing of anything for us eternally. Who shall separate us from any true Love?

August 24. On the summit of Moosilauke.

Have been here four or five days, in cloud and mist and rain. One bright sunset, two pleasant afternoons, on the last of which there was the most beautiful phenomenon that we call "the sun drawing water." I never looked down upon the earth through that many tinted transparency of sun and mist before. It was wide as the whole West, and the tints of green upon the nearer hills were brought out with softest intensity. It was like an open fan of thinnest gossamer, wavering in all possible hues between us and the landscape. But the sign was true. It has rained steadily for three days and nights.

August 27. Monday and Tuesday there was a fine sunset and sunrise, and four travelers were up here to enjoy it. But yesterday the mist and cloud rolled up from the valley again, and in the night a southeast storm set in, preceded by the same sign in the east that was in the west last Thursday. It is one of the signs of approaching rain, — the clearness with which the summits and ranges are outlined through the mist. They are most dreamily lovely, so. I thought yesterday how much the earth and sky were alike, on these high places. It was hard to tell which was mountain and which was cloud.

September 6. A week of great beauty in cloud-scenery, though with little sunshine. Most suggestive phases of cloud and mountain interblending; I have been out in it everywhere I could; twice at sunrise, when I was well rewarded by the glory in the east. The days seem so short! I was foolish to bring books up here, — and yet I have found them companionable now and then. "God in his World" I have re-read — it is a book for the heights.

February 4, 1891. Boston. In my room at the Hoffman House these last two weeks. I could not get settled earlier; others were occupying it. But I love this room, because I have lived so intensely and deeply in it; because I have had revelations in it of God and his truth, of human friendship, of the inmost meanings of life. The very walls seem alive to me sometimes. Every place where we have met God, and come to feel Him as the reality in all things, is holy ground.

One of the pleasant things of the last month was my visit to Wheaton Seminary, and the meeting with Mr. Brooks there, and hearing him speak to the girls, making them more happy, and helping them much, as I have to-day heard. His presentation of Christ as the Way, the Truth, and the Life, has led one, at least, to a decision for herself, that Christ is the Son of God. I like to meet new friends in my old haunts. I have lived through some painful and some delightful experiences at Norton, struggling and groping in solitude through formal dogma and doctrine into spiritual truth, for there was none with me, and my way of thinking was accounted heresy. But I felt beckoned into clearer light than there was around me, and I followed in silence. I first read Maurice there, and F. W. Robertson, who opened doors for me which have never since been closed. And I taught my pupils, giving them what I had received, truths which I felt were unquestionable, and I knew, while there, that it was not wholly in vain, though I had access to but a few. Now I go back, and I find the whole school apparently ready for this clearer spiritual light, and I am glad. We must love places where we have truly lived, — even in heaven we shall remember them.

I finished my little book last week, — "As It Is in Heaven." I wonder if it was presumptuous in me to write it? But it seemed to grow by itself, and I wanted to give the blossoms and fruit that had shaped themselves in my mind, to those who might enjoy them, and perhaps get some refreshment and strength from them. I trust it will be of service to somebody.

April 3. Lent has passed, and Passion Week, and Easter. All these festivals now mean so much to me, and yet not wholly for themselves, but because they make the whole year sacred. I have attended all the morning services, and have found it good to begin the days with that half-hour of prayer and thought, and communion with others. Once I should have thought this frequent assembling together day after day, and week after week, for religious services, at least unnecessary. But for the deepening life that has come to me through them I can never be sufficiently thankful, and I feel that the Church holds through them a special power over the spiritual life of the community. For the last weeks of winter and first weeks of spring, everybody is reminded that this life of ours belongs to us through the life and death of Christ our Lord. We are always forgetting that, — always falling back into ourselves and our own petty interests and plans and thoughts of and for ourselves.

I cannot see why Churches of every name should not keep Lent and Good Friday and Easter, as they do Christmas, and I believe they are moving in that direction.

I was present at the Good Friday evening service at the Old South, presided over by its pastor, Rev. Mr. Gordon, where a Baptist, a Unitarian, a Congregationalist, and three Episcopal clergymen took part. It was most impressive, and seemed like a promise of the time when all Christ's people shall be one. The Good Friday sermon at Trinity Church in the morning was to me a new unfolding of a thought that has always perplexed me, from the text, "The blood of Christ cleanseth from all sin." I could never make the "Atonement," as set forth by the religious teachers of my youth, a reality to myself; Christ Himself was always real, as a divine man, and as a living presence with us still, but how His death was to us more than His Life, I could never see. The grandeur of it all, — the love that inspired the sacrifice, always moved my being to its depths, but the prominence given to His "Blood-shedding" seemed unnatural.

It was tragic; pictorial; yet somehow outside of me — a scene upon which I gazed, and wondered, and longed to understand.

I cannot recall the words of Mr. Brooks's sermon, but the feeling and the thought left with me from it was that now I could see it all; and that through that completed sacrifice, the divine life entered into every human soul that could open to receive it. And it is the very thought of the blood, which represents, and *is*, the life, that made it clear.

He gives all of himself that He has to give, in first living for us, and then dying for us. And the giving means our receiving His pure life into our stained souls, so that their defilement is cleansed, and we live His life of love and sacrifice, instead of our old selfish and sinful one. It is now His blood that flows through us, and inspires us with eternal strength. And this is what it means to be His, and one with Him; the character, the person, must be renewed, when filled with his purity, with his righteousness, and his consecration. Any other view of the atonement than this seems to me still to be something of a fiction. But this view is so inspiring to me, that the cross has a new meaning, — it is the true and only emblem of Christ's work to hold up before the world.

May 17. Mr. Brooks's election as bishop has followed almost as the natural sequence to Bishop Paddock's death, and it has seemed to be demanded quite as much by the community at large as by the church. The feeling has been, that if there is a place of higher influence for such a man, he must be put in it. I have not been accustomed to think that there can be any higher place than that of a Christian minister, but he will not cease to be this. But for me it is like the closing of a beautiful book of inspiration, from which I have been reading for the past ten years, almost constantly of late; and before the bishop's death, I have felt that it was more than any one congregation ought to have to itself, and God will broaden the stream of the water of Life now into more far-reaching channels. The change has brought great sadness, but our best is given us to share, and we shall find joy even in this sacrifice.

May 1. At Beverly, — and tired with my spring languor, and some inward depression. Yesterday I talked with Mr. Brooks about the change that is coming, and though I believe it best and needful for him, still I feel in it an unutterable sadness. It is strange that I do, for I never expect to see him often, or to hear him preach except for a few weeks in the winter. But I suppose we have all had the satisfaction of knowing that the fountain was flowing and that we might drink if we would. And what have I not received at this source? What a different world it is to me, from what it was ten years ago. How I have become strengthened through and through, to see and know what spiritual life is, and in my measure to live it, as I believe! Soul and eyes and heart and hands and feet have been given to me anew, through the illumination received.

That strange "light in light" that seemed to glow around me, as I knelt in reconsecration of myself, a little more than a year ago, has not left me, though it is dimmed by this present regret, and I shall walk on in it through paths yet untried.

Yesterday I sat in the same room and the same chair where, eight years ago, Mr. Brooks first suggested that my place might be in the Episcopal Church. I had not thought it possible, and did not see it so then. To be sitting there in his study, where I had not been again since that first talk with him, as one of his people, and to hear him speak of the strangeness to him of his own new outlook upon life and work, — of the suddenness with which the change has come to him: "First it seemed impossible, and then it became inevitable," he said, — brought back that other day and all the time between, and my own experience in being lifted out of my old associations into the Church, — for it seems to me that unseen hands at last lifted me into my place.

Well might he speak of that room as a sacred room, where so many souls had been strengthened and led on into light. I wish he need not leave his house when he becomes bishop; it is so truly identified with his life. Our place is partly ourself. I am sure he needs a change, after so many years of incessant service, doing the work of twenty men, apparently. He will still have hard work to do, but it will not be of the same kind.

I do believe that the hand of God is in his election as bishop. It is not so much the Episcopal Church (much as he loves it, and believes in it) that is to be benefited: the whole church — the whole community — will feel the difference in the freedom and depth of spiritual life that can but radiate from such a man, wherever he goes. I do want to live at least ten years longer, to have a part in the good time.

Mr. Whittier writes to me: "The very air of Massachusetts is freer and sweeter, since his election," and these are the words of a seer.

And still it is a haunting regret that I shall no longer hear his words in the old familiar way, at Trinity Church.

TO MRS. S. I. SPALDING.

BEVERLY, MASS., June 3, 1891.

MY DEAR FRIEND, — I do not think the weather would have kept me here quite, last week, but I also have had to call myself half-sick. I think it must be the "grippe" or the effect of some subtle seizure of that fiend, for I am unaccountably good-for-nothing, in many ways. I had to lie still all last Sunday. I *must* go to Boston next Sunday, for it is the Communion Service, which has become very dear to me, and more so *now*.

Perhaps I will try again this week coming to you on Friday and going to Amesbury on Saturday for a call; thence to Boston. If you should hear that Mr. Whittier had gone to Portland (he is expected there next week) perhaps you will let me know by Friday morning.

I should *prefer* coming to see you when I could stay over Sunday. But while Mr. Brooks preaches I want to improve every chance of hearing him. I thought he would not be permitted to leave Trinity Church — I believe that he was himself surprised at his own nomination. But he would have fallen in the harness there: no man could do *forever* the superhuman work he was doing, and the collapse might have been sudden. I have seen him within a week or two, and he looks at the new work with all the enthusiasm of a boy. The change may prolong his strength and usefulness; for nothing but change of work would be rest to him.

The *little* side of Episcopacy is making itself manifest, as it must, when so great a man is brought into contrast with *mere* systematizers, petty planners of the Kingdom which is infinite, *so* infinite that it absorbs them, as the atmosphere does motes and insects.

Yours with love,

LUCY LARCOM.

September 13, 1891. Summit of Moosilauke. I have been here three weeks yesterday, with rainy or cloudy weather most of the time, and a few days of perfect beauty. It has been warm weather, never cold enough for winter clothing, but heavy and damp sometimes. In every bright interval I have been out, half a dozen times out in the sunrise alone (one of the best things up here). The sunrises in which the sun was not visible were loveliest; when the rays reached across from under a cloud, and over the lower mists, to the distant mountains in the south, penciling them with soft rose and pearl tints. The finest sunrise was when the sunbeams shone down from under a dark purple cloud on a foamy sea of white mist that covered the landscape, touching its upper surface with the splendor we usually see from below. There was a sunset the night before, with a similar effect, just as a storm was rolling away. There has been less variety in the phases of cloud-beauty than usual.

Yesterday was my best day of all. I walked over to the East Peak, and looked down into the great ravine, where the shadow of our mountain was slowly ascending the opposite slopes. The higher peaks behind shone in soft purple through the rosy mist, and as I stopped at a crest half-way to the Peak, they grew so beautiful in their loneliness, uplifted from sombre depths to luminous height, and brought to my thoughts such heavenly-human associations, of the great ones known and unknown, who have glorified my life and uplifted it into spiritual splendor, that my eyes were again and again filled with warm, happy tears. God has been very good to me in these latter years, in bringing me to the mountains and giving me friends. It is the utter loneliness that I sometimes have with nature, up here, that makes the place so delightful to me. The people are only incidental; only now and then one who loves the mountains in my way, or in a better way, gives them a new attraction.

The mountains are more human to me than any other exhibition of inorganic nature; they are indeed presences. There must be something like them in heaven.

I go down to-morrow, to hotel-life for a week or so, but the peace and strength of the hills will remain in my heart.

Beverly, October 17, 1891. These last three weeks, — these last three days, especially, — have been so full! I have lived more in them, in the very deepest part of my life, than in as many years, often.

The consecration of a bishop whose ministry has been more to my spiritual life than that of any other minister; the joy of knowing him as a friend; the sorrow of losing him as a minister; the thankfulness that I may be counted in as one of his people still, to work in his larger field with him; the certainty that God has called him to do more than ever for the coming of His Kingdom: it is a great flood of regret and triumph that has been flowing through me, and that fills me still. I am full of tears and song; I never felt life so real and so deep. It is like setting sail on the grandest voyage of hope, with a chosen spirit of God at the helm, and all of us full of the inspiration of his life and faith.

I was glad to sit a little aside at the Consecration Service, and feel more than I could see, though I saw all the best of it, — that grand manhood in the midst of white-robed clergy and bishops, one with it all, and yet so superior to it all, the great humble man, bowed among his brethren, to receive his new office! And I shall never forget my first glimpse of him in his new character, with the Communion cup in his hand, a token of service yet to be rendered; Christ's life still to be poured out for his brethren through his own.

So may our lives all be enlarged and strengthened with his, to serve our Master better, in a wider and deeper service of humankind!

TO J. G. WHITTIER.

BEVERLY, February 24, 1892.

. . . The thought of a present God, who is a personal Friend to every Soul, has always haunted me, and of late years has become more real and close. It seems to me that all truth and peace and hope centre there. It gives new meaning to immortality, and to this life as the beginning of an immortal one. Every year it seems a happier thing to be alive, and to know that I cannot die.

Through *thee*, my friend, I have come to see this very slowly. I have always thought of thee as a spiritual teacher. And then of late years to have had in addition the teachings and friendship of Phillips Brooks has been a great and true help. I thank God that you two men live, and "will always live," as he says to you, and that I have known you both.

When he called at Mrs. Spalding's after seeing you, he told us about the Ary Scheffer poem, and repeated it to us from the words "O heart of mine," through to the end, as he went away, standing before the picture, — "Christus Consolator," which hangs at her parlor door. . . .

TO THE SAME.

BEVERLY, MASS., July 10, 1892.

MY DEAR FRIEND, — I heard of you last in Danvers, but I am not sure whether you are there or not, though I have been trying to get around and see! I have been occupied with various matters which have taken me to Boston frequently, and I have usually stayed with Mrs. Guild, Roxbury.

. . . I do not find myself so strong as usual this year, and my plans for work may all fall through. I think I never had so much that I wanted to do, before. My last two little books have been so widely and warmly welcomed, that it seems to me as if I had only just learned what I *can* do. If I had begun to write from what I feel most deeply twenty years ago, I might have been of some real help to the world. But then I had not had the experience, and perhaps could not.

It makes me very thankful to know that you approve my work. We have so often talked over these matters together. I think the inspiration must be partly, at least, from you. I know that my one desire is for *reality* in the spiritual life, for self and for others. . . .

Beverly, October 16, 1892. This summer has

brought me little time for writing, but much for suffering and thinking. Three months ago to-day my dear sister Emeline left this world; suddenly, — quietly, — just "slipped away," her daughter Lucy says. She made herself ready for church, and sat waiting, — but it was heaven for her, instead. Her going makes more difference to me than the departure of any one else could; for she has been part of my life ever since I was born. She did more to shape my mind — my soul — than any one else did. And yet I differed from her in my way of thinking, upon many things; the deep agreement was underneath, at the spiritual foundations. I think her great power over me was in her great capacity for love. Her great heart, while it was faithful to home ties, failed of love to none of God's children; and to me she was even more mother than sister. Her going makes it an easier thing for me to go, when the time comes.

Then, while on Moosilauke summit, the news of Mr. Whittier's death came to me — more translation than death. I seemed to see him pass on by me, up the heights, and seemed to hear him say, as he passed, "So easy a thing it is to die! Like the mountain blending with the clouds, like the melting of earth into sky, is the transition from life into loftier life." He too passed away in peace; the lovelier to think of, because he had always dreaded the hour of death. He, too, was my noble and tried friend; in my life for more than fifty years. He is associated in my life with the beauty of the hills and the sea that we have enjoyed together, with the deep things of poetry and religion, which were indeed one reality to him. The memory of fireside talks in his own home, with his sister, so dear to us both; the readings of "In Memoriam" with him after she was gone, — are most blessedly vivid to me.

And Tennyson has died, within a week! One could know him only through his poetry, but what a halo that has hung over our mortal life in all its phases! To know the man and the poet, as I knew Whittier, and to be able to feel the greatness of both, is an immortal possession.

Emerson, Browning, Bryant, Whittier, Tennyson, — and where are the singers who take us into the heart of things as they did? There is a delicate murmur of trained voices making music in this modern air, but it does not arrest us and hold us, as the voices of the now silent masters did. It is hardly an age of song.

TO MRS. S. T. PICKARD.

BEVERLY, October 16, 1892.

. . . I have dreamed of him [Mr. Whittier] lately, sitting by the fireside chatting in the old way, as when I used to visit him and Aunt Lizzie. She was more to me than almost any friend, more even than he. I always thought of them as one; and now they are together again. They cannot be far away. I want to keep near them in spirit, so as to find them at once, by and by. I am glad I did not ever know that he was rich. He used to want to pay my bills when we were at West Ossipee, etc., but I declined, for I supposed he was almost as poor as myself, though I know of late years his books have paid well. I am very glad he left me the copyright of the books I compiled with him; and indeed it was only right, as I worked so hard on them. The "Songs of Three Centuries" nearly cost me my health; the publishers "rushed" it so. I was good for nothing for three or four years after, as far as writing went. But he never knew.

TO S. T. PICKARD.

BEVERLY, MASS., November 11, 1892.

DEAR MR. PICKARD, — The trouble with me now is that I am on the invalid list, and am warned not to promise or undertake any new work at present, nor to work continuously in the future, as I have done. The heart seems to be the weak member, and really stops me, even upon slight exertion. I have meant to look over my letters from our friend, and see if there was anything you could use; but they are packed away with others in a cold room, where I do not venture to go. I have not left the house for nearly four weeks, now, and I see that some revolution in my way of living must be made. But I hope to be stronger some time than I am now, — at least to the extent of getting out into the air. I am sorry not to be able to say that I can be depended upon, though I will gladly do what I can to help you.

It is unfortunate for me to be hindered by the state of my health, as I had plans I wanted to set about at once, of my own. It is imperative for me to be earning money regularly, for an income, as I have never quite accumulated it into the thousands. My recent little books, for the past four years, have been more profitable than before, and I can see one or two more as possibilities, if I could put myself down to the work. I mention all this to show you how I am situated, as to doing what you suggest.

Then there is one other thing, — Mr. Whittier many times said to me, apparently in earnest and jest, both, — "Don't thee ever go writing about me!" It used to hurt me a little, as if I would parade his friendship for me in any way! I could not do, after he died, what I would not when he was alive, — unless I knew he was willing, — and he never hinted any wish of the kind, certainly. I have already been asked to furnish "Recollections" for two periodicals, and have declined. I may be over-particular in this matter, but I do feel a delicacy about it, — almost as if I had not the right.

I write just as the matter looks to me now, and with the sincerest wish to honor our dear friend's memory. Tell me your view of it!

Yours sincerely,

LUCY LARCOM.

TO FRANKLIN CARTER.

214 Columbus Avenue, Boston,
January 10, 1893.

Dear Frank, — I have just finished reading the life of Dr. Mark Hopkins, and think it a most interesting record of a grand life. I thank you for sending it to me. I could not help thinking, as I read, how full our country is of noble men of whom we know nothing, or very little. I knew Dr. Hopkins was an able man, but he was only a name to me until I read your book. But of course he was a very unusual man. How grateful and glad you must be that he was your teacher, and that you could tell his story so well! I have known little of you, and you of me, for several years. I have felt that the years of work could not be many for me, and so I have been hard at work writing, that I might give something to those who could receive from me, before I died.

I do not know whether you have seen my little books or not. I have published three in the last two years. The two prose books I thought I had a call to write, and the response they have received has shown that I was not wholly wrong.

Perhaps I have given myself too closely to writing, for I am far from well. Careful medical examination shows that I have organic heart-disease, which will need to be watched carefully in the future; I shall have to go slowly hereafter. Yet I have many plans that I want to carry out; and it is as necessary now as ever for me to earn my daily bread. But I am not in the least bit anxious. The kind of writing I do, does not bring much money, and I am not desirous of writing the kind that does.

These later years have been happy ones to me, because I have been doing things I like to do, and have had noble and sympathetic friends. One of my best friends — Whittier — is out of sight now, but I do not feel that he is far away. Life is one, in all the worlds, and it is life in God that unites us all. God in Christ is the great uniting reality to me. And yet I live so far from my ideal of what it is! How much more we should all be to each other, if we believed it, through and through! —

I cannot write, or do anything continuously, without pain in my chest, so I desist, with love to you and yours.

Faithfully ever,

LUCY LARCOM.

TO MISS FOBES.

ROXBURY, MASS., March 14, 1893.

MY DEAR MISS FOBES, — I did not think it would be so long before your kind letters would be acknowledged, but the truth is that even a little book, if one's heart is in the writing of it, is very absorbing, — and mine has taken all my time. I am reading the proof sheets of it now, and it will be out early in April. (I am visiting a friend here, for a week, trying to rest a rather tired head.)

These little books I have somehow been impelled to write, from the feeling that others might be helped, by seeing the way I had been led, and the point at which I had arrived. For I can but think of these later years as having been most plainly to myself under spiritual guidance. I prayed for it always. I remember walking alone in the woods behind Monticello Seminary, my heart asking with tears that I might suffer much, if so I could find the true secret of life. I have not suffered as many have, — I have only had ordinary trials and losses and matter-of-fact struggles with circumstances, but I have often been in danger of succumbing to lower standards than I believed in. But it has been the one effort of my life to keep in sight the highest and best, and to be satisfied with nothing less.

Now the best seems to me the simplest: — to receive, and to give by living it, the life of Christ. That is the thought I have kept before me in my little book, which I call "The Unseen Friend." I shall send you a copy, as soon as possible.

I am much interested in what you write of the word "eternal." It was on the meaning of that word that my first divergence from the Calvinistic theories occurred, many years ago. I read F. D. Maurice much, and still do so. His rendering of the word "eternal" was, you know, considered heresy in his own church. Now, the exception is, in this region, to hear it preached in any other sense. I think it first implies the *character* of the life, but also its *duration.* It is only the real that can last, and grow better and better forever, as being a progress into the infinite life of God. It is death to refuse to receive this life; I cannot think that any soul will forever refuse, though the freedom of the human will makes it a possibility.

I look upon this life on earth as but a beginning, rather an education than a probation — and yet that also, as every hour of our life is a trial of our fitness for the next hour. One thing I have liked in the Episcopal Church since I knew it and have been in it, is that they preach this practical, spiritual life so much more than systems and doctrines. The Christian year is a repeated following of the story and the spirit of Christ's life, and everybody can understand it. Nobody can hold the Apostles Creed, and not believe in the oneness of the Son and Father, and that is the pivotal truth of Christianity. More and more I see the failures in my past life, through not entering into this central truth in a more living way.

I thank you for the kind things you say of my poems and books. There is no one whose approval I value more deeply. Sometimes I wish I had more years before me, for I feel as if I were just beginning to see clearly, and I am more and more interested in this human life of ours. Yet how little any of us can do to relieve its burdens. How hopeless its evils and sins sometime look!

I have just read "David Grieve." It is far from being a cheerful book, though powerfully written. It is, however, an improvement upon "Robert Elsmere," which seemed to me wordily weak.

I have seen Emily Dickinson's poems, and enjoy their queer gleaming and shadowy incoherences. It does not seem as if her mind could have been fairly balanced. But her love of nature redeems many faults.

That poem in the "Christian Union," "The Immortal Now," must have been printed early in the year 1890, I think. Possibly in 1889, but I believe I wrote it in the winter of 1889–90. If I can find a duplicate, I will send it to you. I have a half-project of collecting my religious poems by themselves, for next Christmas. What would you think of it?

Always affectionately yours,

LUCY LARCOM.

The following letter was written to Bishop Brooks a few days before his death, and was found on his desk, while his body still lay in his home, the soul having gone to be "near the Master and Friend."

TO PHILLIPS BROOKS.

214 COLUMBUS AVENUE,
January 17, 1893.

It is a real trial to me, my dear friend, that I am unable to hear you to-night, when you are probably speaking so near me; and yet a greater to think that I may be denied it all winter. For I find myself more ill than I supposed I was, and am not at present permitted to go out at all. It is a heart derangement, which has shown some dangerous symptoms. I have been to Trinity Church, but am told that I must not attempt walking there again. It seems childish to tell you about it, but you know you are my rector still, — and I had been looking forward to seeing and hearing you occasionally.

Sometimes it seems to me that God's way of dealing with me is not to let me see much of my friends, those who are most to me in the spiritual life, lest I should forget that the invisible bond is the only reality. That is the only way I can reconcile myself to the inevitable separations of life and death. I know that I feel more completely in sympathy with those who went away from me into heaven long ago than I did when they were here. Still I love and long for my friends, and would gladly see them while they are here, in the dear familiar way.

I have accustomed myself to the thought that my call hence may come suddenly, and if I should not meet you again here, you will know that in any world I shall look for you near the Master and Friend in whose presence you live here, and whose love you have helped me to see as the one thing worth living for anywhere. I can truly say that the last ten years of my life have been better and happier than all that went before.

Faithfully yours, L. L.

February 20, 1893. A strange mingled experience the last three or four months. Weeks of illness in the late autumn in Beverly, when I suddenly was brought to the knowledge that I have an incurable disease of the heart, which had been aggravated by overwork and neglect. In the enforced quiet, I could only think, and that was not permitted about disturbing things. Then, a little recovered, I came to Boston just before Christmas, and used my strength too rapidly, so that now I have been in my room under the doctor's care, for over a month. And since I have lain here, a great calamity has befallen. The noblest of men and friends has left the world, — Phillips Brooks. One month ago this morning he breathed his last. He, with whom it was impossible to associate the idea of death; — was? — *is* so, still! — the most living man I ever knew — physically, mentally, spiritually. It is almost like taking the sun out of the sky. He was such an illumination, such a warmth, such an inspiration! And he let us all come so near him, — just as Christ does!

I felt that I knew Christ personally through him. He always spoke of Him as his dearest friend, and he always lived in perfect, loving allegiance to God in Him. Now I know him as I know Christ, — as a spirit only, and his sudden withdrawal is only an ascension to Him, in the immortal life. Shut into my sick-room, I have seen none of the gloom of the burial; I know him alive, with Christ, from the dead, forevermore. Where he is, life must be. He lived only in realities here, and he is entering into the heart of them now. "What a new splendor in heaven!" was my first thought of him, after one natural burst of sorrow. What great services he has found! How gloriously life, with its immortal opportunities, must be opening to him! He, — one week here, — the next there, — and seen no more here again. The very suddenness of his going makes the other life seem the real one, rather than this. And a man like this is the best proof God ever gives human beings of their own immortality.

I treasure my last memories of him, the last sermon I heard him preach at Trinity, at the October Communion; the last time I saw him there, just before Christmas, and the last warm pressure of his hand, and the sunlike smile as he spoke to me at the church door; the last note he wrote me when he spoke of Mr. Whittier in the other life, with such reverent love: "Think what — *where* — he is now!" — even as we are thinking of him. It seems as if God gave me these last three years of intimate friendship with him, in connection with the Church, as the crowning spiritual blessing of my life. The rest of it must be consecrated to the noblest ends, like his.

In March and early April, 1893, Miss Larcom's heart-trouble was rapidly developing into an alarming condition, and she realized that the end must soon come. Her life had reached its climax in the little book, "The Unseen Friend," in which she had written her last and greatest religious message to the world. More of her friends were on the "other side" than here, and her eyes eagerly sought the visions beyond.

Her old pupils and friends remembered her during those weary days of suffering in the Hoffman House, Boston. Her beloved niece, Miss Lucy Larcom Spaulding (now Mrs. Clark) was with her constantly, ministering to her needs. Some sent her flowers, which she loved so dearly; others, fruit; one desired to send from the West a luxurious bed; and one sent a reclining-chair. The old cook, Norah, at Norton, asked the privilege of making graham bread for her. Her old scholars remembered her more substantially, by a loving gift, in those days when her pen was forced into idleness. She painfully felt the restraints of her illness. Her nights were full of distress. In a half-amused way, she said, "I never knew what it was to be really sick. I knew people had to stay in bed, and have the doctor, but I thought they slept at night."

The end drew near. On Saturday evening, April the fifteenth, she said it would be a great joy to exchange the physical for the spiritual body; and she was comforted by reading Bishop Brooks's addresses, "Perfect Freedom."

On Monday, April the seventeenth, she grew rapidly worse; and in her unconsciousness, she frequently murmured in prayer, the word "Freedom."

On this day her soul was released, and she entered into the fullness of the Glory of God.

On a little slip of paper she had written these last words: —

> "O Mariner-soul,
> Thy quest is but begun,
> There are new worlds
> Forever to be won."

She was borne lovingly to Trinity Church, where she had worshiped; and there, in the presence of her sorrowing friends, the service was held. There was also a service in St. Peter's Church, Beverly, where her fellow-townsmen gathered to do her this last honor. She was laid to rest in the soil of her native town, within sight and sound of the sea.

INDEX.